# A Simple Path to a Better Life

P L A N
U N D E F
C H A R G E
P L A Y
O R G A N
S E E K
I G A G E

## BRENT GALLAGHER
### with Steve Knox

# Note to the Reader
## The 7 Week Journey to Discover Your Purpose

Discovering your Purpose is a journey of being honest with yourself, deep reflection and casting vision for your life. This is why we designed *Purpose* to be read over the course of 7 weeks.

Following each chapter there is a reading guide that walks you daily through the chapter with questions to help you get the most from this book. These questions will provide structure for your discussion as you read each chapter with your spouse, significant other or small group.

# CONTENTS

# INTRODUCTION: What if...?

What if I told you by the time you finish reading this book, that you would hold the keys to unlocking your purpose in life? What if I told you that by discovering your purpose in life could help you change your health forever and feel energized throughout each day? What if I told you that you could help combat one of the world's biggest epidemics of all time in childhood obesity? What if I told you that you could become a better version of yourself in 7 short weeks?

What if....?

It's challenging to ask "What if?" Those two words cause us to step back and challenge the current accepted thinking of our times. Throughout history those two words have challenged traditional thinking –

- *What if the world is round?* - Christopher Columbus
- *What if we put a man on the moon?* - President J. F. Kennedy
- *What if we could access the world in the palm of our hand, through a mobile phone?* - Apple Founder Steve Jobs

These individuals challenged the statue quo, and refused to accept life "as is."

Everyday you wake up you get the amazing opportunity to ask "What if...?"

---

What if you….

- packed your lunch today instead of eating out for the third time this week?
- focused on getting quality sleep every night as opposed to running tired all day only getting 5-6 hours on a good night?
- stepped back and discovered what you want your life to stand for instead of chasing the latest fads promising the world?
- cared as much about your personal health (weight, fitness level, wellness) as you do for the health of your career and bank account?
- were honest with yourself and others and realized that you're not giving 100% effort to living a healthy life… instead of secretly blaming it on a lack of time, a slow metabolism, stress, tiredness, kids, a busy schedule, work, not enough hours in the day or the laundry list of other excuses you continually make.

"What if…?" is only the first step in on the path to discovering your purpose and becoming a better version of yourself. Real change requires action. When it comes to your health and well-being, you can be like the masses making empty promises always saying that you'll handle it tomorrow, next week, next month or even when the New Year rolls back around. As the old saying goes, "You never step into the same river twice." The same holds true for your life. You will never get a second chance to relive today. If you are sick, tired and/or depressed due to being out of shape, overweight and fueling your body with 'fake' processed food, you are not alone. Most of America is addicted to the wrong foods, spending billions of dollars annually on quick fixes that don't work, wasting time, energy and resources that they don't have.

What if you took action today? What if you drew a line in the sand, turned around 180 degrees, and walked the other way? What if you changed?

What if you cleaned out your cabinets and refrigerator of all the processed foods and started fresh again? How much temptation would be gone from your house?

What if you took a cooking class, just four times a year, to learn 5 new healthy dishes to prepare for your family? How could 20 new healthy meals a year help change the health of your family?

What if you planned out your dinner menu the weekend before and bought only the foods needed? How much money would you save not wasting foods that go bad?

Living a fit and healthy life is not rocket science like the magazines, TV shows, infomercials, and trainers to the stars are selling you. There's no secret sauce, special training techniques, or fad diets that will have you dropping amazing amounts of weight before the week is over. You already know everything you need to know to lose weight, eat healthy and feel energized. You know that you should move more, eat real (straight from Mother Nature) food, and focus on getting quality sleep. You know that you should cut back on the processed foods that are filled with countless so-called 'healthy ingredients'. You know that taking a pill isn't really going to melt away the fat from your mid-section or your thighs. You know that "rewarding" yourself daily is not part of a healthy eating plan.

It is time that you stop lying to yourself. It's time that you own up to the personal choices you make. It's time to stop making excuses for the unhealthy life you choose to live. I say it's a choice because no one forces you to stay in bed, skip your workout, purchase unhealthy and processed foods, drive everywhere, take the elevator, sit all day long, or believe the hyped-up marketing you see on TV or in the magazines you read regarding your weight loss or health.

Look back on one big purchase you've made in your life: a car, house, engagement ring, college, etc. How diligent were you in this process? You probably researched a lot. You probably asked questions. You probably were a bit skeptical when answers were given. Your health is no different. If sitting around all day had an immediate impact on your life, as opposed to crippling you years later from neglect, you would do something about it...today. If eating poorly almost everyday instantly gained you the 5 lbs, you would rethink the choice you were about to make. If skimping on sleep and caffeinating your way through the day caused you to have that heart attack sooner rather than later, 7-8 hours a night would become a high priority.

To change your health, drop inches, reduce blood pressure, increase energy, and let's be honest, look good naked, it's time you start taking personal responsibility for your actions. To begin taking the first small in regaining your health, you need to discover purpose in life - something bigger than yourself worth living for. At the end of the day, you want your time here to stand for something and to have a direct impact on those you loved most. To live your life to the fullest and to be able to leave a lasting legacy, you have to maintain a healthy body.

Throughout these pages, you will walk through 7 small steps that you can apply daily to your life. Regardless of whether you are just starting out or a seasoned fitness enthusiast, looking to drop 63 lbs or trim down the last 4, this book will provide the answers and the inspiration for the journey you are on.

These 7 small steps are pretty simple, but don't be fooled, they are powerful when put into practice. Simple sounds too true to be good, but you don't have to reinvent the wheel, you just have to use it for it's original purpose.

Define your purpose. Live your legacy.

# CHAPTER ONE:
## *PLAN: Clarifying Purpose*

*"Put your ear down close to your soul and listen hard."*
                                        - Anne Sexton

I lost the final game of my college soccer career in the conference finals 1-0. It was a heart breaker, but when the final whistle sounded we were defeated. My official career as a soccer player had just ended. There was no "next game" or even "next year." I was finished. My goal from as far back as I could remember was to train and be good enough to compete at the collegiate level. I stood on the field frozen and paralyzed, because I did not know what life would be like without soccer.

To be honest, I thought my ride of competitive soccer would never end. I had not thought past that final game. What was I going to do without it? No more training, no more games, no more team trips or good laughs after practice. The loss of friendship and camaraderie was almost too much to bear. I had played for almost 20 years of my life, and now it was over. Sure, I had accomplished my goal of playing soccer in college. But what was I going to do next?

My goal to play college soccer had been fulfilled but I was not satisfied. Instead of soaking up a great life experience, I was lost. I had no purpose going forward. I had lived my life to accomplish my one and only goal and now it was fulfilled. I went into a bit of a funk.

Running helped fill the gap – my search for purpose - in my life. I was like Forrest Gump. I started to run. And run. And run. I never looked back. Running was a way out for me. It was a release of adrenaline, but it was also a way to avoid facing the decision of what I was actually going to do with my life. I would avoid friends and family with the simple excuse "I can't. I have to run tomorrow." Running became my drug of choice. It overtook my mind and soon overtook my body. I needed my fix everyday. I needed it so bad that I never took a day off and chalked it all up to, "I need to run. I'm training for a marathon. That's what marathoners do - we run."

It would be an understatement to say that season of my life was a lonely time. I used to talk about my long runs with my friends. It always made me feel good when they would say how crazy I was for doing it. This only fueled my fire to run more and run longer. I was addicted. I lined up marathons left and right. What I did not realize at the time was that even though I was running thousands of miles, I was actually going nowhere in life.

To the casual observer, I was fit. I could crank out 6-minute miles like it was nothing. A 3-hour marathon - check. A 10 mile run after a day of classes and an hour in the weight room - check. Absolutely destroy the buffet line at the 'Caf' with so called "healthy" foods - check. I was a machine by all definitions. *But was I truly healthy?*

Every morning I woke up, my ankles and knees ached. Everyone close to me said I needed to chill out and enjoy life more. I gorged on processed carbs - pastas, cereals, pizza - like there was no tomorrow, because I needed to keep my intake of "carbs" up so I could run more. I pushed away loved ones in my life. I secretly battled depression. I started taking the weight loss drug Ephedra because I was looking to get even leaner, go faster and go farther - I was about 160 lbs at the time. I quickly dropped to an unhealthy 138 lbs and looked like a bag of bones, but I was still searching for the perfect body that I had pictured in my head.

But hey, I was fit. I was skinny lean. I was the talk of my friends when it came to health and fitness. In my head, I knew I was traveling down the wrong path. But on the outside, I kept up this facade because I needed something more. I needed a purpose for my life. And at the moment, my life revolved around the rush of endorphins I got from grinding it out on the pavement. I never really fully understood that I pushed away everyone who had ever cared for me all because I was lost.

Then one day I took a small step in a different direction. I began to search for a deeper purpose for my life. I began to reflect on the time that I had spent investing in the lives of young athletes coaching and teaching them the fundamentals of soccer. Seeing them grow had a significant impact on me. One kid in particular stands out in my mind, as he was a good, polite and hard-working player with a lot of potential. I remember he always shook my hand after practice and thanked me for the session. This kid was a bubble player with potential to move from the 2nd team to the 1st. I knew if he put in the work on and off the field and had the support and encouragement from his parents, he could make it. Two seasons later he did. It was during that time that I began to realize that I enjoyed helping people develop and grow to become better.

## A DREAM COMING TRUE

I had dreamed for 6 years of creating a training facility that simply *helped people become a better version of themselves.* The idea wasn't revolutionary. It wasn't new and improved. It wasn't the next get fit gimmick or fad diet. It was based on timeless principles - living with purpose, being honest with yourself about your habits, and finding the joy in playing again. I wanted people to start thinking more about training to live rather than living to train. But how was I going to open a business based on becoming better when I was secretly addicted to the "runners high?" What woke me up from my addiction to over-training was the reality that I was not practicing what I preached. I had replaced my joy with an addiction.

On Sunday, January 15th, 2006, I completed my last marathon. It was the Houston Marathon, one I had completed three times. I got the t-shirt, the medal, and treated myself to a massive breakfast of French toast. As I settled down later that day, I began to think about the following day. It was going to be the biggest Monday of my life. It was the day I had dreamed of for 6 really long years. I was set to open my training facility at just 26 years old.

Then I thought, "You're a hypocrite, Brent! How can you open a business to teach people about finding *the joys of playing* when you don't even practice what you preach?"

On Monday, January 16th, 2006, as I placed the keys in the door to unlock and open for the first time, I took a moment to say a prayer. In that moment, a sense of peace fell over me. I knew what I had to do to be successful - *become a better version of myself...*

There are some definite extremes when it comes to personal fitness and health. My story is one extreme where discipline crossed the line into an unhealthy obsession. Countless others are at the opposite end of the spectrum where lack of discipline has crossed the line into apathy and indifference. Both extremes are unhealthy, and I believe both extremes are the result of a lack of clarity in understanding our purpose.

## WHAT'S YOUR PURPOSE?

The first step in becoming a better version of ourselves begins with understanding our purpose. Once that is identified, we have a clear picture of where we are headed. But we have to do more than just envision a better future for our lives. We have to actually cultivate a *plan* to bring that vision into reality. This means setting meaningful goals and working hard to achieve them. We cannot go it alone so we must find honest accountability folks that will challenge and encourage us along the way. Most importantly, it means taking responsibility for our lives and taking action.

If we are going to make any lasting change in our personal health and wellness, then we need to be motivated by something deeper, something more significant. Real change doesn't happen overnight. It takes time, energy and hard work. Lasting change takes significant commitment. It requires us staying the course and overcoming setbacks. In order to change our behavior and lifestyle, I believe we need to discover the internal motivations that actually drive our behavior. We need to identify a cause bigger than ourselves to fight for.

For some of us it is as simple as being healthy enough to play with our kids when we get home from work. For others it might be increasing our mobility so that we can regain some personal confidence to be a part of the world again. Some of us have traded in our health for success in the business world. We are far beyond where we thought we would ever be in regard to our ability to actually enjoy what we worked so hard to achieve. The bottom line is that there is a better way to live.

The opposite of action is atrophy. 'Use it or lose it,' is not a cliché, it is the truth. We have to get serious about our choices. When we say, 'Oh, this cheeseburger won't do us any harm.' Or, we say, 'We'll start exercising tomorrow.' We are just making excuses for our behavior, and actually heading away from achieving our purpose. Excuses only delay the inevitable and complicate our problems. When we make excuses today about our health we are crippling our future hopes and dreams. Tomorrow becomes next week, month or even next year, and we pretend to not understand why we are constantly tired, cranky or sick? How many more poor meals do we have to have before we wake up? How many years will we go feeling tired and stressed out without taking responsibility for out health? Life does not have to be this way.

## BIG PICTURE PROBLEMS

There is an old expression that says imitation is the sincerest form of flattery. But in the case of children becoming overweight and obese like adults, it's not very flattering at all. Why? Out of the 30 adults we walk past or see each day, 20 of them will be either overweight or obese. If we look at our local pre-school, we will notice that a quarter of the children are either overweight or obese. If we were to visit any grade school playground we would notice that one-third of these children are either overweight or obese. It is scary to think that adult obesity rates have doubled since 1980. Even more eye-opening is that fact that the obesity rates of our children have more than tripled in the same time frame.

The 2013 US population is 314,800,000. Of this nearly 315 million population, roughly 100 million have the ability and drive to keep themselves healthy enough to maintain a 'normal' body weight. The remaining 200+ million Americans walking around are either overweight or obese. Let's look to see how this is playing out in our daily lives:

- U.S. hospitals are ripping out wall-mounted toilets and replacing them with floor models to better support obese patients.
- The Federal Transit Administration wants buses to be tested for the impact of heavier riders on steering and braking.
- Cars are burning nearly a billion gallons of gasoline more a year than if passengers weighed what they did in 1960.
- Disneyland reconfigured the "It's a Small World" attraction to accommodate a generation of riders who were too

large for the original cars. New roller coasters now routinely include seats or rows designed specifically for the extra large.

- Almost 27% of individuals applying to the military can't get in because they weigh too much.
- Kids are now starting to develop adult type of chronic diseases - diabetes, high blood pressure or cholesterol, depression, and even heart disease - due to carrying around too much extra weight.
- Since 1977, the consumption of sugar-sweetened beverages has increased by 135%.
- More than 75% of Americans drive to work - a 300% increase since 1960.
- In 1969, 42% of kids walked or biked to school. Today, more than 80% are driven to school.
- Almost 55% of food consumption happens outside of the home.
- Restaurant portions are 2-5 times what we physically need (research shows when we're served more we eat more).
- The average American is eating and drinking 600 more calories per day than they did 20 years ago.
- Bagels 20 years ago were only 140 calories and 3" diameter, today they are 350 calories and 6" diameter
- Cokes 20 years ago were only 85 calories and 6.5 oz; Today they are 250 calories and 20 oz
- French Fries 20 years ago were 210 calories and 2.4 oz; Today they are 610 calories and 6.9 oz

These are the stats, the by-product of a consumer driven society. So who's to blame?

## PERSONAL RESPONSIBILITY

We want to point our finger so we can avoid taking personal responsibility for our actions. If we point and look outside ourselves, we can still feel good about living an unhealthy lifestyle. We can still feel good about choosing the fast food option over the home cooked healthier one. We can still feel good about saying "I'm too tired to get up and move" as we flop down on the couch after a day of sitting for 8+ hours at work. We can still feel good about neglecting the small daily healthy choices we can make to turn our health around. We can still feel good about accepting the status quo for our own lives, while we secretly admire those who are going out and making the local community, state, nation and world a better place.

We have to take one small step to educate ourselves about living a healthy life. We can't rely on the TV or social media to tell us the truth. Businesses exist to do one thing: make a profit. There is nothing wrong with that, but it does mean you have to be proactive in your choices. The only person truly looking out for the goodness of your health is you. The largest marketing dollars will go to products that have the highest profit margins - which typically include the highest processed foods and are the primary culprits in our obesity problems. The profit margins from a soft drink are as high as 90%, while fresh produce is only 10%. We have to pay attention.

We must teach by doing. Doing means role modeling nutrition and exercise habits that lead to a healthy life. Think about it this way: On average we are blessed to wake up in the morning 30,000 times during our lifetime. If we are 26, we still have about 20,000 mornings left. If we're 54, we still have 10,000. Our lives can change in a heartbeat. We have to make the most of every opportunity to pass along the wisdom in which we live by. This is our life; let's not miss a day of it.

As parents, leaders of schools, coaches, mentors - just about each one of us - we have the responsibility to educate ourselves in child and teen nutrition in order to set a good example of what it means to live a healthy life. Research has shown that parents who are overweight are much more likely to have children who are overweight. This makes sense when you think about the fact that the family usually eats the same foods and have the same attitudes about exercise.

*This is why purpose matters.* When we discover our purpose we are not only taking responsibility for our own lives, but making a significant choice that will impact future generations. We can literally change our family tree with one small step.


## THE WAY FORWARD

In order to live a life of purpose we have to have a sense of urgency about the importance of even the smallest task, planning our day, preparing ahead of time and anticipating adversity. Small steps acted upon consistently propel us into achieving our goals. A life of purpose requires getting back to the basics, starting small, working hard, and taking responsibility for our choices. A life of purpose requires intentionality and accountability. A life of purpose requires a plan.

All of us have plans: weekend plans, business plans, weight-loss plans, travel plans, and retirement plans. Yet very few of us take the necessary steps to achieve what we have set out to do in the first place. Over promising and under-delivering has become a way of life for so many of us. In order to break the cycle, we need to create a simple and achievable plan that we can begin to implement today.

I still have a business plan that I wrote in college. That plan was not overly complex or complicated, but it worked. That simple plan has guided me as I built my business, managed my time, made financial decisions, and invested in my employees. When

I wrote it, those that advised me, wanted to make it so complicated, and I asked myself, "Why do we complicate life?"

The truth is we like to complicate life, when all we really need to do is to find what works and keep working it. There are principles out there that help us if we will simply apply them, persevere, and stay the course. I have found that some of the most profound and life-changing truths we will ever discover are very simple. In our modern day culture, we worship the complicated and the sophisticated. Some believe that simple ideas are not profound, that instead, simple ideas are only for kids. Nothing could be farther from the truth. I have met with many fit and healthy individuals, and in almost every case they keep their training and nutrition philosophies uncomplicated. My philosophy is the same healthy advice your grandmother would give to you:

*Keep it simple.*

*Keep it clean.*

The word "plan" in Latin literally means "foundation". This carries with it the idea of a blueprint or groundwork. Here is a working definition:

*A plan is an intended outcome achieved through specific goals over a certain period of time.*


## AN INTENDED OUTCOME…

It does us no good at this moment to try to define our fitness goals. They are shallow and don't allow us to look inwardly and express our true purpose in life. The 'fitness goals' question typically summons up brief answers such as "I want to get in shape," or "I want to lose weight." They are honest but the answers are vague realities to our true reason of wanting to become healthy. These answers lack an emotional response. If we think about it, emotion has been the precursor of virtually every life-altering decision we've made. If we truly want to become a better version of ourselves we have to start with our own passion and desires.

If we want a great life, and I believe most of us do, we have to challenge ourselves by asking deep questions. Questions that can help us begin thinking about our own stories, experiences and purpose in life. But we have to be true to ourselves. We have to start with the end in mind. There are two questions that we can ask that will help us define our purpose:

1) What legacy do we want to leave behind?
2) How can being fit and healthy help us achieve this legacy?

Legacy is about the future. Legacy is what we leave behind for those that follow us. Deep down all of us want to be remembered well. We want for some part of who we are and how we have lived to impact the next generation. We long to make our mark on history, to leave the world better off because we were here. Legacy is the belief that quality is more important than quantity. Legacy is the ability to take responsibility for the people, places and resources that we have been entrusted with. Legacy is a life marked by hard work, generosity, and faithfulness.

Legacy is the realization that life is about relationships. We have a relationship with our spouses, our children, our family, our coworkers and our friends. But, we also have a relationship with the food we consume, the energy we use and the time we spend. Like the hub and spokes of a bicycle wheel, all of these connections come back to the center. They come back to the core of who we are as individuals.

When I think about legacy, the first face that pops into my mind is that of my Grandfather. His life was marked by curiosity, generosity and passion. To say he was larger than life would be an understatement. My mother's father was a WWII pilot who loved planes. So much so that when he started his business he chose a location next to the regional airport so that he could be by planes every day. Flying for him was about gaining a different perspective, seeing the world in a different way. He wanted my mom and her brother to be curious about life. The curiosity, generosity and passion of my grandfather created a legacy that has impacted and shaped me in ways that I cannot even express. That is what legacy does. It is a force of good in future generations.

At our core we need to connect. When our relationships are out of whack so are we. When we live disconnected lives, we actually are settling for less than the life we were created to live. The strength and health of these connections determine the depth of life that we experience and impact that our lives will have and legacy we will leave behind.

## PURPOSE EXERCISE #1 – Legacy

Answer the following questions in the space below…

1. What is the *legacy* you want to leave behind?

2. How can being fit and healthy help you achieve this legacy?

## ACHIEVED THROUGH SPECIFIC GOALS...

The word "goal" was originally used to describe a limit or boundary experienced in life. It has evolved over the centuries to have multiple meanings. Specific goals find their origin in what we care most about. When we care about something, we take action. And with action comes momentum. That momentum has the power to change the choices we make, our health, our body, and helps us live a life full of purpose.

Goals are milestones along the journey to fulfilling our purpose. Goals are tangible markers that represent our perseverance and faithfulness to becoming a better version of ourselves. Goals are a way to track and celebrate the blood, sweat and tears of this journey that we are on.

Setting specific goals is all about starting with the end in mind and working backwards. By breaking down the overall purpose into measurable chunks we can begin to formulate the steps that we need to take in order to define and achieve our goals.

Fear is one of the biggest obstacles for us in achieving our goals. Both the fear of failure and the fear of success hinder us from moving forward and acting on the goals we set. The fear of failure is rooted in the past. The fear of success is rooted in the future. If we set goals and don't achieve them, then we just continue the cycle and pattern of who we have always been and we prove the naysayers right. The fear of success is even more powerful though, because if we set goals and actually succeed, then we are forced to move out of our comfort zone and actually take the next step and grow. Either way, facing our fear is a fundamental part of accomplishing our goals. Fear is a natural human emotion, and anytime we are experiencing life, taking risks, or moving outside of our comfort zone we will undoubtedly have to deal with our own fear.

Another obstacle that stands in our way of achieving our goals is the broken record of our own excuses. Our excuses are the verbal procrastination and avoidance of pain. These are the little lies that we tell ourselves in order to place blame and avoid taking responsibility for our actions. The opposite of making an excuse for our behavior is acknowledgement and ownership of the choices that we make. In order to stop lying to ourselves about our health and behavior we need a bit of humility to admit where we are and how we got here. All of us have made excuses for our poor behavior along the way. If we truly want to change and achieve our deeper purpose we need to be honest with ourselves. We need to begin to live in reality.

In order to set goals that are specific we must we clearly identify and track our progress. This is not a new principle; however, it is something that very few people put into practice. It is one thing to know the right thing to do. It is an entirely different thing to act on what we know. This is the difference between theory and practice, and with practice comes progress.

Specific goals are easily understood and measured. A simple goal is easy to define and track. Again we don't have to overcomplicate the process. We don't have to set a goal of climbing Mt. Kilimanjaro to get motivated. Having the energy and mobility to play in the backyard with our kids is a great goal. Simply by moving more, we can positively increase our health.

Goal setting is a matter of starting small and building momentum gradually over time. Goals should stretch us but they shouldn't break us. One thing I try to encourage and teach all of my clients to do is to move 30 minutes a day. Move. Walk, hike, run, play…it does not matter. Move. Get active and stay consistent. There's no infomercial or sales pitch here. If we move just 30 minutes a day we begin to see results. Every journey begins with the first step. If we continue to take small steps in the same direction, over time we will reach our destination and will undoubtedly lay the foundation for a life lived with purpose.

## PURPOSE EXERCISE #2 – Goals

What 3 simple goals can you set this month to becoming a better version of yourself?

- I will…
- I will…
- I will…

## OVER A CERTAIN PERIOD OF TIME.

Socrates said that, "the unexamined life is not worth living." Working towards goals over a set period of time is all about tracking our progress. When we measure ourselves, we know how far we've come and how far we have to go. When we have a blueprint and roadmap for where we hope to go, we give ourselves the best chance to reach our destination. Deadlines should be renamed Lifelines, because when we reach them we are actually creating growth and vitality.

I first met Laura when she had been referred to see a trainer because of a physical ailment called frozen shoulder. One of the first conversations I had with her was about her health and fitness goals. Like most of my clients her answers revolved around losing weight and her current health issues. We created a simple plan with short-term goals that would give her the confidence to keep taking the next step. She agreed to come in for 30 minutes twice a week for a month to work with me. That month turned into a year, and that year turned into two. It all began when she committed to a certain period of time.

Over time as our relationship grew Laura came to a place where she opened up about the fear she first felt walking into the gym, a single mom feeling overweight and depressed. She revealed that what kept her coming back was the process of taking small steps with the encouragement and support of me as her trainer. The deeper purpose for Laura was becoming healthy enough so that she could have the energy to be the best mom to her two boys and a role model to her friends and family. Achieving her goals was possible because of the small successes that she had experienced along the way. She not only lost the weight and gained the physical strength, but she also discovered her purpose with the mental and emotional strength to keep taking the next step. Laura walked into our gym with a frozen shoulder, and today if you asked her, she would say that the weight of the world is off of her shoulders.

Laura is a perfect example of how discovering personal purpose and creating a simple plan with specific goals can transform lives. Laura's successes have not only changed her life, her choice to become a better version of herself has had a ripple effect in the lives of her family and friends. When we discover the impact that being fit and healthy can create in the lives of others, it becomes a catalyst for staying the course and establishing the legacy we long to leave behind. Our determination, hard work and sacrifice inspire others to become better versions of themselves.

## PURPOSE EXERCISE #3 - Ownership

My PURPOSE for becoming fit and healthy is…

# *Chapter One:* PLAN: Clarifying Purpose Review

*"What man actually needs is not a tensionless state but rather the striving and struggling for some goal worthy of him. What he needs is not the discharge of tension at any cost, but the call of a potential meaning waiting to be fulfilled by him."*

- Viktor E. Frankl

## <u>Week One Reading Plan</u>
### Reading / Reflection / Result

**Monday**
- Read Chapter One

**Tuesday**
- What is the legacy you want to leave behind?

**Wednesday**
- How can being fit and healthy help you achieve this legacy?

**Thursday**
- Re-Read Chapter One…

**Friday**
- What is your biggest obstacle to achieving your Purpose? Why?

**Saturday**
- What stood out to you the most from this chapter? Why?
- What are you going to do about it?

**Sunday**
- Rest

# CHAPTER TWO:
# *UNDERSTAND: Rethinking Food*

*"The belly rules the mind."*        -Spanish Proverb

Fad diets do not work.

Quick fixes and fads eventually go as swiftly as they come. In 2011 Americans spent $61 billion dollars on dieting, with $3 billion of this spent on diet pills alone. There are an estimated 70 million Americans who start and stop diets annually. Yet we are still heading toward obesity at an ever increasing rate every year that goes by. Why?

Fad diets are not sustainable over a lifetime.

However, healthy eating habits are sustainable. What we truly need is a deeper understanding of the purpose of food. There is no doubt that we are a culture obsessed with looking and feeling better. If we really do want to change we need to rediscover healthy eating habits. We need to redefine dieting and look at our choices that shape our lifestyle. We also must take an honest look at our relationship with food and educate ourselves on what will allow us to become a better version of ourselves.

To say, "We are *what* we eat," is really a misnomer. In reality, we are *why* we eat. When it comes to achieving the health and fitness that is going to allow us to fulfill the purpose we discovered in the first chapter, we have to connect the dots between our diet and our purpose for becoming a better version of ourselves. What we eat is important, but it is the tip of the iceberg when it comes to discovering the unhealthy behaviors that are driven by *why* we eat what we eat.

Purposeful eating comes from understanding our relationship with food. In the last chapter we examined the alarming rates of obesity in the American population both in adults and children. A recent USA Today article noted the fact that 13 of the 50 States are 60% obese. Obesity in and of itself is a preventable disease. The costs involved in education and prevention of obesity are a fraction of the cost of treatment. The Center for Disease Control recently estimated that the cost to the U.S. for obesity alone is currently $190 billion dollars annually. Add to the list diabetes, heart disease and other weight related health issues and we can see that our relationship with food as a nation is totally out of whack. To say it is an unhealthy relationship would be an under-statement. Our relationship with food is deadly. We have to take responsibility to educate ourselves and take back our health and secure a meaningful future for ourselves and our children.

John joined our gym and signed up with one of our train-ers because he wanted to lose weight. Initially he dropped nine pounds of fat fairly quickly by adding regular physical activity to his weekly routine. A few months into his training he hit the dreaded wall – a weight plateau – where nothing changed for weeks. John could not understand why he was not seeing the con-tinued results that he had experienced when he first started work-ing out. He was still training five days a week, conditioning on some days and hitting the gym on the others. Though he pushed harder in his workouts, the scale would not budge.

After much frustration, his trainer asked him, "Have you made the changes to your food intake like we discussed?"

John was taken aback. He hadn't really made any changes to his diet at all. He saw the early results that came from training five days a week and assumed he could sweat the pounds away. Moving from inactivity to activity was not enough to achieve the results that John was after. His body quickly caught up with the amount of physical activity he was doing and the food he was consuming. The result was inevitable - the weight loss stopped. John's number one problem: he had a fixed mindset. He wasn't ready to make a change in his food intake.

Like a lot of us, John wanted to try to out-train a bad diet. What he discovered was the painful reality – our relationship with food determines our level of health and fitness. When we're honest with ourselves – when we own up to *why* we actually put certain foods into our mouths (when no one is looking or will ever find out) that is when we will begin the journey of achieving the health and fitness we desire. If we want to change, then we have to take responsibility for the person we are becoming – fit or overweight. Ninety percent of the battle, when it comes to our health and fitness, revolves around our relationship with food.

## FOOD FOR THOUGHT

The marketing in commercials are geared to sell us lies that only lead to early graves. We are up against a multi-billion dollar machine when you consider that there is a 90% margin of profit on fast food, whereas fruits and vegetables have a 10% margin of profit. The food industry does not want us to eat meals based on our values. They are serving up low-priced, low quality "Value Meals" targeted at our fast-paced, convenience-driven lifestyles. Eating to change our mood or behavior has become a natural pastime that is fueled by big food companies that are only concerned about their bottom line. We have to stop and ask, "Who is reaping the real value here?"

When we eat to fill the void or hole in our life, we typically do so with comfort foods. Comfort foods may make us feel better in the moment, but really they are just a temporary fix to a deeper issue. We can never fill the psychological void with a physical prescription. We end up com*pounding* our problems. Emotional eating is a response to a deeper psychological need. The main reason to eat is to satisfy hunger, but so many of us eat as a reward, a stress relief or to be comforted. We have to ask ourselves if we are emotional eaters.

## FOOD EXERCISE #1 – Answer the following questions:

Do you ever eat to feel better? Why?

Do you ever use food as a reward? Why?

Do you ever eat when you are already full? Why

Do you ever eat food secretly? Why?

Do you ever feel controlled by the food you eat? Why?

Does food make you feel secure and comforted? Why?

Food is…_____.

We can begin to understand our relationship with food when we clarify the difference between genuine and emotional hunger. Genuine hunger is driven by a natural craving for the food our body needs. Emotional hunger is typically triggered when we experience some type of *dis*-comfort. We turn to food to comfort ourselves, and when we do we usually are ruled by an impulse of instant gratification with some sugar-loaded snack. Genuine hunger is quenched when we are full. Emotional hunger is never quenched no matter how much we eat. When we are deeply honest about why we eat what we eat we begin to peel back the layers on our motivations. Our motivations are driven by real and felt needs that are both physical and psychological. By examining our relationship with food we can gain a deeper self-awareness into our health and wellness.

Webster defines addiction as, "the state of being enslaved to a habit or practice or to something that is psychologically or physically habit-forming." Typically, when we talk about addiction our minds immediately go to drugs, alcohol or tobacco…but what about sugar, salt and fats? Our bodies have been programmed to enjoy them. Sugar, salt and fats make things taste great. But when asked, "Are they healthy for us in mega doses?" What would our answer be? Since the early 1800's, the average American's overall amount of sugar intake has increased more than 1,500 percent. Cancer at the turn of the 20th century affected one in fifty, now it affects one in two. Is this just a coincidence? We are self-medicating through foods loaded with sugar, salt and fats that might feel good in the moment, but are crippling us in the long-run.

We should be addicted to the foods that are good for us. The foods that are actually good for us come in season and go out of season. We were not designed to have whatever we want whenever we want it twenty-four hours a day, seven days a week. Fifty short years ago we had to eat what was available during that season. Our bodies were designed to need different foods in the summer, fall, winter and spring (That's why they call it 'seasonal fruits and vegetables'). We have fallen out of tune with the natural rhythms of our diet as human beings. In times past we would get our fix on healthy foods, like broccoli for example. When it was in season we would eat it, when it was going out of season we would have had our fill.

If we do find that our relationship with food is out of whack, it typically means that at our core we still have some questions to answer in regards to our purpose. When we introduce healthy habits to replace our unhealthy ones, we begin to move towards becoming a better version of ourselves. In order to turn the tide when it comes to emotional eating we must pay attention to *when*, *where*, and *what* we do when we fall off the wagon. Most of us self-sabotage in response to stress, boredom, anxiety and lack of proper sleep (We will look at this more in depth in a later chapter). Again, it is up to us to be responsible, that is, in choosing foods in those moments of weakness that are good for us. If we turn quick fixes filled with high sugar, salt, and fats into real whole foods filled with nutrients in those moments of vulnerability, we will move towards health and wholeness.

Our bodies know when they are getting real food. It's as if there is a switch in our brain when we actually eat something that is good for us. We fill up and feel up when we do so. The alternative is the sick-cycle which is an indicator of a deeper problem that food just cannot remedy. Artificially sweetened foods leave us empty. Eating whole foods makes us whole. When we look at fruits, vegetables and grains we can see that these are whole foods. They have integrity in the sense that the outside matches the inside. If we buy a banana then we know we're getting the fruit on the inside of the peel. When we buy a box of processed fruit snacks we have no idea what we are actually eating.

Our bodies would actually crave the right things if we had not conditioned them to be addicted to foods that were bad for us. We naturally crave fats, sugars and salts. Food companies know this fact – so they pump in sugars, salts and fats to almost everything we eat. Back in the day when we started craving something sweet we would eat honey. Today we reach for a candy bar, Coke or a box of chocolates to quench the same craving. It is almost impossible to find a product under 5g of sugar in our local grocery stores. Breads, soups, diet drinks or canned goods (basically anything in a package) are crafted to make us want to consume more of them. The end result is that we become addicted to them. Once addicted, we lose the natural craving for foods that are actually good for us. The sugars we get from an apple just don't taste as sweet anymore. We have traded the natural system of healthy eating in exchange for an instant gratification artificial diet.

## BACK TO BASICS

Eat more frequently. Eat smaller meals. Don't eat after 7:00pm. Take this pill. Eat low fat, high fat, less fat. Eat more carbs, less carbs, high protein, or less protein.

It seems that we are no better off than a dog chasing his own tail – circling around and around, but never truly getting any closer to solving the main problem. We are missing the point here. Again, simplicity is best when discussing food. Food was originally designed to fuel our activity. We can stop chasing the latest diet fads in our quest for health and vitality and get back to the basics and build our nutritional foundation on foods that will actually fill us up the right way. We know that a healthy diet includes:

- fruits, vegetables, and whole grains
- lean meats, poultry, fish, beans, eggs, and nuts
- healthy fats, probiotics, and lots water

There are 5 foundational food groups: proteins, carbohydrates, fats, vitamins & minerals, and water. Most diets focus on eliminating one of these essential food groups, but in reality we need all 5 of these if we want to live a healthy and productive life.

We must have the right amount of protein in our diet. Protein builds, maintains, and replaces the tissues in our bodies. We also need the right carbohydrates for energy. Carbs are the most basic form of fuel for our bodies. Our body breaks carbohydrates down into simple sugars, which are absorbed into the bloodstream via insulin where the sugar we eat can be used as a source of energy. Our diets must also contain healthy fat. Dietary fat is used to fuel the body and helps us absorb some vitamins and minerals that we need. Probably the most overlooked and essential element of a healthy diet are eating foods that contain the right amounts of vitamins and minerals, also known as micronutrients, that our bodies need. Micronutrients are different from proteins, carbo-hydrates and fats because we only need them in small doses to maintain health and wellness.

One cause of overeating is the lack of a proper nutritional in-take built upon high quality micronutrients. In keeping the main thing, the main thing; we can stop chasing the latest diet fads in our quest for health and vitality by getting back to the basics and building our nutritional foundation on the small micronutrients found in vegetables, fruits and whole grain foods.

Eating real, whole food provides you with the vital nutrients need to allow normal body growth, development and function. The nutrients, that come from a eating real, whole food, assists in fighting diseases and infections, as well as keeping our skin healthy. Nutrients help us lose weight, stay energized, fight blood pressure and cancer, as well as increasing cardiovascular health.

We all have our fair share of excuses as to why we don't eat healthy foods more consistently. According to a national poll in the June 2012 issue of ShopSmart magazine, these are the top excuses (that's right – EXCUSES):

57%: Eating healthful foods is too expensive.
47%: Social settings are too tempting.
39%: Life is too short; I want to enjoy what I eat.
33%: It's hard to find healthy options when eating out.
29%: I don't have the time to prepare healthy meals.
25%: My family prefers less healthy meals.
20%: Unhealthy habits are too hard to change.
18%: Healthy foods don't satisfy my appetite.
13%: I'm not sure which foods are healthy.

The number one trump card we have to gain control over all of these excuses is applying the knowledge we already have. We view eating healthy as expensive because we've fallen victim to massive portions of cheap, low-nutrient foods we can purchase for $0.99. Big gulp's, king-size and value meals are all products of profit maximizing decisions the big food companies make so they can get us to purchase more – the key to them staying in business and remaining profitable.

It's interesting that, "not sure which foods are healthy" was at the bottom of the list. That's because we know what's healthy and what's not. We don't need to learn anything new about food. We just need to take action and apply what we already know about eating healthy. We need to be intentional everyday, by choosing to take the small daily steps needed to begin eating healthy. We can invest in our health now, or pay the price later in doctor visits, hospital stays and a lifetime worth of medicines and chronic disease. The choice is ours.

Basic nutrition also demands that we hydrate properly. We can survive up to 4 weeks without food, but only 3-5 days without water. Water is essential for our bodies to function properly. It is a catalyst for our metabolism. Water regulates our body temperature, protects our organs and tissues, lubricates our joints, carries oxygen and nutrients to cells and reduces the burden on our kidneys. Our bodies are made up of 60-70% water. Our brains are 79% water. Needless to say, proper hydration matters if we want to be healthy and fit.

A 2011 study from the University of Washington revealed that 75% of Americans are constantly dehydrated. They also discovered that 37% of Americans regularly mistake dehydration for hunger. The researchers also discovered that dehydration was the main factor in everyday fatigue, slow metabolism, joint pains and headaches. Factor into the equation that in 2011, Americans set a record in bottled water purchases of an estimated $11 billion dollars spent and drank 9.1 billion gallons of water. That is an estimated 29.2 gallons of bottled water per person according to sales figures from Beverage Marketing Corp. But, sugary drinks sales have also increased with a resulting increase in obesity rates in America.

Understanding our need to properly hydrate can significantly relieve back and joint pain for up to 75% of folks who suffer from these issues. If you consider that if we have just a 3% drop in body water it can cause a lack of cognitive abilities resulting in short-term memory loss and our ability to focus on our daily tasks. The benefits of proper hydration do not stop there. If we would simply drink 8 glasses of water every day we would decrease the risk of colon cancer, breast cancer and bladder cancer.

## SIZE MATTERS

Our obsession with convenience and consumerism has gotten out of control, but it does not have to be this way. We can choose today to change. There is more strength in us than pressure around us, if we tap into a deeper reason for living. The size of our heart is what really matters. When we understand our passion for life and purpose we will begin to take a hard look at how much we're eating. Instead of letting restaurants and marketers decide how much we need to eat, we can make educated choices based on what we really need to live a better life today.

Most Americans know that portion sizes have increased over the years, yet a lot of us do not connect the dots between the amount of food we eat and the effect it has on our overall health. For instance, the standard size plate used in restaurants has increased from 10 ½ inches to 12 inches just to accommodate our current craving for more food and larger portions. Our plate size and waist size are directly related. Researchers have found that we tend to eat most or all of what we are served, rather than taking leftovers home.

Most of our daily caloric intake is from soda and sugary drinks. Artificial sweeteners are hidden in most of the beverages we drink. Companies add calories to beverages that are not always obvious to consumers looking at the list of ingredients. Some common caloric sweeteners are high-fructose corn syrup, fructose, fruit juice concentrates, corn syrup, sucrose and dextrose. The best way to cut down or avoid these calorie-loaded beverages is to simply choose water. Most of my clients say they do not like just drinking water. One way to make drinking water more palatable is to add a slice of lemon, lime, watermelon or add a bit of real juice from our favorite fruit. We don't have to totally stop drinking our favorite beverages, however, we have to limit the serving size of these beverages. By adopting an old-school mentality of moderation we can head towards health and wholeness and still enjoy our favorite drinks.

Since 1950, our caloric intake has increased on average to an additional 294 calories per food item. For example, instead of consuming the traditional 8 oz coffee with cream and sugar at 45 calories, we're now downing a grande latte loaded with sugar and fat at a whopping 360 calories. Less really is more. Portion control alone can affect how much weight we gain or lose on a weekly basis. By cutting out a simple 500 calories a day (3,500 calories in a pound of fat) we could lose an estimated 1-2 lbs a week on average.

## SIMPLE STEPS

Blake is a performance coach on my team at my training facility. His journey to eating healthier is not that uncommon, even coming from someone who is in the health and fitness industry. Since his story is basically a series of taking small steps, I asked him to share:

I made a decision that changed my life. Growing up I was a very active kid, full of energy, and had a bottomless pit for a stomach. I could eat anything in sight! But I was a very picky eater. My diet consisted of eating Hamburger Helper, pepperoni pizza, hot dogs and BBQ...and absolutely no vegetables. My diet lacked any nutritious value; in fact I wouldn't even give bright colored foods a try! If it was green, it was not going to touch my plate, however every meal had a dessert waiting for me once I cleaned my plate.

Recently I became aware that I was lacking the energy and drive that I used to have in my college days. I was convicted by the fact that I was no longer full of the energy I once had in my youth. In that moment I knew I had to make a decision if I was going to be able to fulfill the dreams I wished to achieve. That day I flipped the switch and made a commitment that has changed my life.

My new goal was to try new healthy foods, specifically, green foods! This sounds relatively easy, but for me this was a huge step considering the only green thing I had ever eaten were green beans and pickles. My mission was to "Go Green".

I set out small and simple steps to get started: I would eat a piece of fruit and something green every day for lunch. Again, this sounds easy, but for me it was a real challenge. I was willing to give anything a try to see if it would help me regain the energy and drive I used to have in college. So my start was adding a small plain salad to every lunch with some vinaigrette dressing. I still remember the first time I took a salad back to work for lunch. Everyone looked at me in confusion wondering who the salad was for. After a few weeks of following through on my commitment they soon found out that I was a new man.

The next step I took was adding other healthy nutritious foods to my salads. First carrots, then spinach leaves and I even began to add cashews. My new salad was slowly becoming a big pile of nutrients. The really crazy thing was that I actually started to become excited about my next lunch. I discovered that "going green" was actually a fun experience now that I had so many different ways I could eat my salad. I stuck with my plan. Some days I would choose a salad with Quinoa, and other days it would be with beans. I just kept varying my salad toppings from day to day, to not burn out and to keep it fresh and new.

Over about a month's time I began to feel the best I had felt, even including my days back in college. I soon realized what my diet was missing even back then – brightly colored nutritious foods. By making one small change to my diet and sticking with it I felt like a new and improved me. I was more energetic throughout the day, I had more confidence in the way I looked and felt. The bottom line was that I was happy with my decision to "go green" and this rubbed off on others closest to me to join in on this new way of life.

Regaining my energy started with a small committed step towards becoming better. The small easy steps that I took I knew could be accomplished with dedication and determination. My on-going results: I feel great. I'm losing body fat and sleep better at each night. All it took was a desire to truly become a better version of myself, a simple plan and the determination to stay the course.

Blake's story is a great illustration of becoming self-aware about our food choices and how simple changes to our diets can drastically improve our quality of life.

When we look at the types of food we eat we can see a pattern emerging over time. Remember, our choices are shaped by our values. By going back to our purpose for becoming a better version of ourselves we can have the internal motivation to move towards health and wellness in our everyday food choices. Awareness is about taking an honest look at the choices we make. If we were to take pictures of our meals for a solid week in a digital food journal what would we see? What are the color's of the foods? What portion sizes? What food groups? What would be missing?

Awareness is essential, but it is just information if we do not act on what we see. Preparation is paramount if we hope to change our eating behaviors. We live most of our lives reacting to life rather than proactively influencing it. This is clearly seen in our relationship with food. We waste our resources when we do not slow down enough to take the time a plan ahead.

In a recent study done by the FDA about 25% of food purchased by Americans is wasted. According to the study, the process of delivering food to our kitchen tables takes 10% of the total U.S. energy budget, utilizing 50% of U.S. land, and consumes 80% of all available fresh water in the U.S. The troubling fact they uncovered was that 40% of food in the United States today goes uneaten by families and households. They estimate that this is more than 20 lbs of food per person every month. Even more disturbing is the fact that Americans are wasting about $165 billion each year on uneaten food. There is a correlation between how much food we waste and the size of our waists.

At home we have taken this to heart. The food that we buy from the grocery is perishable. We limit purchasing food that last for months at a time; we buy food that lasts only for days. As opposed to shopping for weeks at a time, we plan out what food we need to buy for the week at hand and eat accordingly. This accomplishes two things for us. First, it ensures that what we eat is the best, freshest and highest quality food available to us. Second, it forces us to be intentional in planning our daily meals. The result is that we have an accurate estimate and balance of what we need and what we eat. This is a simple way to regain control of our eating habits and food budget. One other simple principle that we've adopted over time is that we mainly shop around the perimeter of the grocery store. We do this for multiple reasons, but primarily to avoid processed foods that are loaded with unhealthy amounts of fats, sugars and salts.

Our refrigerator looks somewhat empty. This is by design. We only keep on hand what we're going to eat that week. Again, we have planned this in advance. On our counter at home is a basket of fresh fruit and two-tiered basket full of veggies. This is by choice, because we know that what we see is what we're going to eat. Most homes in America have massive refrigerators and pantries that are filled with all the wrong foods. It's as if we're stocking up for an apocalypse. We are all for living within our means and creating a budget that is planned and proactive, but some of us are lured in by deep discounts on snack foods, sweets and junk food. Again, we need to remember we are more likely to eat what is readily available. The law of scarcity applies here: if it is not on hand we simply cannot eat it unless you get in the car, drive to the store, purchase the food, drive home and then finally eat to fulfill your graving (Sounds silly, doesn't it? But we're not addicted are we?).

There is a marketing principle here. We have no control over where product placement is when it comes to the local grocery store. Companies pay big bucks to have their products at eye-level on every shelf in every town across America. Marketers know that we are driven by sight. We eat what we see. If we flip this in our favor and put healthy foods in arms reach on our counter tops and kitchen tables, then we will be more likely to reach for them instead of for any unhealthy alternatives. If all that is available is our foundational foods – fruits, vegetables, nuts and grains – we will adopt a habit of healthy eating.

Food companies also know that we live hectic lives and don't have time to read the fine print. Most food labels mislead consumers. Knowing that we are a health-conscious society, major food companies have used the FDA rules to their advantage. "Reduced Sugar" equals artificial sweetener, which has been linked to cancer and other negative health effects. "100% Whole Grain" doesn't always mean 100% healthy. "Gluten-Free Donuts" always make me laugh. And the list goes on..."Heart Healthy," "Smart Baked," and "Fiber-Enriched Pretzels" just to name a few other popular smoke and mirror techniques employed by the big food companies. Educating ourselves on what is really healthy is important if we want to regain control of our lives and live with purpose.

Where do we start?

## PUTTING IT ALL TOGETHER

The majority of excuses associated with taking action revolve around our time and our money. As we discussed in the first chapter, when we don't live life on purpose we spend most of our time reacting to life instead of influencing it. We have more power to impact our future, and the future of our children than we actually know. When we live a life of purpose we gain clarity through awareness and we gain responsibility through intentionally choosing to live differently. We can always come up with an excuse not to change...it's too expensive, we're too busy.

The reality is that when we eat on purpose and with intentionality we feel better, think clearer and have the energy to accomplish more throughout the day. We have to start with the end in mind, and ask ourselves if making the sacrifices and changes to our diet in order to become healthy and fit enough to achieve our deeper purpose is really worth it?

If we are going to change our diet, we have to change our behavior. In order to change our behavior we have to ask ourselves *why* we eat what we eat. This is built on a clear understanding around our relationship with food. Awareness and preparation move us towards sustained healthy choices and living when it comes to our diets. Taking stock of our lives (and refrigerators) will help us come up with a simple plan that is achievable to accomplish our goals of being fit and healthy. Self-discipline is a by-product of self-awareness, and that is why real and lasting change happens when we act on what we know about ourselves at the deepest part of who we are as individuals. When we are fit and healthy we will have the energy and mindset to live a life of purpose and leave a legacy of impact.

## SEVEN TIPS FOR HEALTHY EATING

We want to make eating healthy food really complicated. Maybe it's because we feel that it can't really be that simple. Maybe it's because we think that if we make it complicated, then we have an excuse as to why we're not eating healthy. Maybe it's because we want to believe everything we hear on TV or read in a magazine when it comes to "magically" losing 10 lbs in a matter of days. Maybe it's because … excuse after excuse after excuse.

I recently sat down and thought through what I thought were the simplest and most honest ways to eat healthy. I came up with 7 easy Food Principles:

- **DOWNSIZE:** It's proven that the bigger the plate, bowl, spoon, fork, and serving utensils you use, the more you eat – up to 77% more in some cases over small options. A simple example is to use your dinner plate for a salad and vegetables, using your salad plate for main dish.
- **CHECK THE LIST:** You can't scale back your portions until you come to grips with how much you're really eating. Look at the serving size of your next 'treat'. It might look innocent, but when you realize that there are 3 servings in

one tiny package, it just breaks your heart. Look for stuff with one ingredient – apple, carrot, almonds, etc.

- **EAT BREAKFAST:** Eating breakfast increases fullness and reduces hunger throughout the day. There's a reason they call it the most important meal of the day. Don't like to eat breakfast – start with something small. Eventually your body will begin to feel hungry as soon as you wake up.
- **SLOW DOWN:** Research states that more chewing results in an increased release of hunger-quashing gut hormones and lower levels of gherlin, a hormone that stokes appetite. Slow down a bit and enjoy your food more. Facebook, twitter and all things media will still be there when you return. BONUS: The slower you eat, the less food it takes to feel full.
- **GET OUR ZZZ's:** Sleep-deprived subjects feed themselves 300 more calories a day than when they were fully 7-8 hours rested: 2 x week for a year = 8 lbs of fat. Plus, a lack of sleep causes you to crave food more – NO not the healthy kind either. How to start – create a dark & cool bedroom. Wake up at the same time everyday – even on the weekends. Take your phone out of the room – every time it buzzes, it wakes you out of sleep, which is the only time your body has a chance to fully recharge.
- **UNDERSTAND MARKETING:** Research found people eat 28% more when a item was labeled "low fat." When something has been altered from it's original version (low fat, fat free, reduced fat, sugar free, no sugar added, fiber enriched, gluten-free, etc) they have to put something else in to make up for what they take out. Typically, a low fat food has almost the same amount of calories as the original. There is always more sugar. It's time we see through the crafty messages designed to falsely lead us to believe

the chemically laced products are healthy and good for you.

- **EAT REAL WHOLE FOOD:** Start eating real food - vegetables, fruits, lean meats, etc. It's processed as little as possible, close to its natural state, free of additives and it can be farmed. Protein bars and drinks are marketing tricks. That simple. If you have to ask if something is real food, then it probably isn't.

Eating healthy doesn't take a degree in nutrition or sitting down with a Registered Dietitian. All it takes is common sense. You're smart. You wouldn't be where you are today if you were not. All you have to do is to apply that same wisdom to the food you fuel your body with.

Start small. Be wise. Live with purpose.

# *Chapter Two:* UNDERSTAND - Rethinking Food

*"If more of us valued food and cheer and song above hoarded gold, it would be a merrier world."*
— J.R.R. Tolkien

## Week Two Reading Plan
### Reading / Reflection / Result

**Monday**
- Read Chapter Two

**Tuesday**
- What do you need to rethink about food? Why?

**Wednesday**
- How can healthier eating and food habits help you achieve your legacy?

**Thursday**
- Re-Read Chapter Two…

**Friday**
- What is your biggest obstacle when it comes to food in achieving your Purpose? Why

**Saturday**
- What stood out to you the most from this chapter? Why?
- What are you going to do about it?

**Sunday**
- Rest

# CHAPTER THREE:
## *RECHARGE: Maximizing Energy*

*"Energy and persistence conquer all things."*
- Benjamin Franklin

Work-life balance is practically a myth.

Work is a means to an end, and not the end itself. When we live purpose-filled lives we understand what we are fighting for and what it is going to take to achieve our goals and leave a legacy that matters to future generations. But how do we sustain this type of life? How do we not burn out (if we haven't already done so) on the quest to achieve what we want to accomplish? How do we persevere for the long haul?

If we are going to cross the finish line in a healthy way, then we need to learn how to *recharge, refocus, and relax.* We need to understand what it means to live a healthy rhythm of life by managing stress and getting proper amounts of sleep. We also need to be honest about our own hectic schedules and take a deeper look at why we are working so hard in the first place.

We are told that stress and fatigue come with the territory when it comes to being employed in America. Fatigue takes it's toll on us both physically and emotionally weakening our immune system, causing us to become more susceptible to serious conditions like heart disease, depression and other illnesses. In a recent Bureau of Labor Statistics study it was estimated that U.S. workers spend more time at work than any other developed country in the world. Factor in the difficult pressures of what economists are calling the great recession, where we're earning less and working more, and we can clearly see the toll this is taking on our bodies.

40 short years ago the average work week for US workers was 35 hours, today it is over 45 hours. Call it a good ole American work ethic, but most of us work more than that, based on our availability to be accessed via all the technological advances like laptops and mobile phones. We check work emails and answer calls at home and work on the go. One recent work survey estimated that, on average, a US worker spends an additional 7 hours a week working after they are technically off the clock checking and responding to emails. Needless to say we are wearing ourselves out physically, emotionally and mentally.

Those of us who work more than 40 hours a week are 6 times more likely to 'burn out' than those that work fewer than 35 hours a week. Recent research conducted by the Aragon Institute of Health Sciences in Spain revealed that working long hours increases the risk of long-term exhaustion, a loss of interest in our work and high levels of irritability. Needless to say, that if we burn the candle at both ends without sufficient recharging time, we will eventually burn out.

In the past 20 years, Americans have taken less vacation, worked longer days and pushed back our retirement dates by an estimated 7 additional years. We have become accustomed to grinding out long hours decade after decade. Most of us get two-weeks of vacation which we use to spend time with family that doesn't really give us the break we need from our hectic schedules. A common post-vacation comment around water coolers everywhere, "I need a vacation from my vacation." On average the US is one of the most vacation-deprived nations. We are overworked, under appreciated, underpaid and sleep deprived.

Being driven is not a bad thing. Hard work and discipline are great American qualities. Pulling ourselves up by our own boot-straps through blood, sweat and tears are the stories we celebrate, but at what cost? Could there be a healthier way to achieve the goals and dreams we have for our careers and our families? The good news is that we do not have to live this way; fatigue and restlessness are treatable and preventable.

## SHUT EYE

Not only are we getting away and taking fewer vacations annually, we're also getting less sleep than our grandparents. On average Americans are getting less than 7 hours of shut-eye a night compared to the 9 hours on average that our grandparents maintained. Technology and hectic schedules complicate matters for us and limit our ability to get the full 7-8 hours that are optimal for functioning at our best. When we slow down and get the proper amount of rest, we actually achieve more. If we think of our bodies as energy engines and the right amount of sleep, healthy food and exercise as the fuel, the equation becomes quite clear. Most of us are running on empty the majority of the time.

## RECHARGE EXERCISE #1 – Answer the following questions:

**How many hours of sleep do you average per night?**

**How rested do you feel?**

**When was the last time you truly felt refreshed?**

Sleep is one of the most important parts of the equation. It seems counterintuitive that ceasing to work actually makes us more productive, but by making it a rhythm of our days and weeks we can actually increase our productivity at work, focus on the task in front of us and have the energy to finish what we started. If we do not make sleep a priority we end up paying the price during our waking hours.

There are five stages of sleep that we pass through from when we close our eyes at night to when we wake up in the morning. These stages progress at regular intervals from the first stage through to REM (Rapid Eye Movement) then begin again with Stage One. A complete sleep cycle takes an average of 90 minutes depending on age, weight, diet and other factors. Our first sleep cycles each night have relatively short REM stages and long periods of deep sleep. Later at night our REM stages increase and our deep sleep stage decreases.

In Stage One of our sleep cycle we experience a light sleep where we technically drift in and out of sleep. We have all experienced this at some point while driving for long periods of time. When we feel that in and out of semi-consciousness we are actually in the first stage of sleep. In this stage, everything slows down including our eyes and major muscle groups. It is in this stage, that a lot of us experience muscle contractions and a sense of weightlessness.

In Stage Two our eye movement actually ceases and our brain activity becomes slower. When we enter Stage Three of our sleep cycle we experience a series of slow and fast brain waves that are extended over and over again during this stage. In Stage Four our brain produces what are called delta waves, or slow brain waves, and this is where our body is significantly at rest. Researchers believe that it is in Stages Three and Four that we enter what they call "deep sleep." It is during this time that when we are woken up we feel groggy and unresponsive. In deep sleep, there is no eye movement or muscle movement.

During the REM Stage our breathing becomes more intense and irregular, our eyes move rapidly and the muscles in our arms and legs are momentarily paralyzed. Our brain actually kicks back into gear at the same level as when we are awake. It is in the REM Stage that we dream and experience nightmares the most. Healthy people getting the recommended 7-8 hours of rest a night actually experience three to five sleep cycles of REM sleep. Studies show that infants spend almost 50 percent of sleep in the REM Stage, and adults spend nearly half of nightly sleep in Stage Two, and the other 50 percent between the other four stages.

Our bodies were designed to need a certain amount of rest each night in order to function properly. The amount of rest each of us needs every night varies. The average adult needs approximately 7-8 hours of sleep each night. Most of us will stay up late or get up early, but very few of us have regular healthy sleeping patterns. Unfortunately, this runs our body down making us more susceptible to sickness, viruses and diseases because our immune system is not functioning at its best due to fatigue. When we get the right amounts of rest our body performs as it should, but when we don't we pay the price. According to the Center for Disease Control, 40 million Americans suffer annually from some type of sleep disorder which costs their employers some $18 Billion dollars to loss in productivity and other issues. Sleep is serious business.

When I first got married, my wife and I were on different sleep schedules. I was not a real night owl, but she definitely preferred to go to bed earlier than me. This didn't fly for very long, because she was used to getting more sleep than me. The first few months we would go to bed around 10pm and I would cut the light out after reading. She began to ask me to cut the light off at 9:45pm, so I did. A few months later it was 9:30pm. A few months after that it became 9:15pm and then 9:00pm. Before long we were in bed every night by 830pm. I had become an early bird and learned something in the process.

I used to think that my energy was high enough that it could not get any better. I thought my body was fully charged for the busy day I had ahead and sleep was not that important. To be honest, I thought I was bullet-proof and never felt I needed more sleep. But when I started sleeping longer at night it did not take me long to realize that I had been only fooling myself. The difference that 90 minutes made on my energy level was incredible. I felt fresher in the morning and had a greater energy reserve throughout the day. It was a slow change that I adopted over time.

I have learned to plan my sleep schedule to fit according to my early training time with my clients at 5:30am. I typically wake up at 4:00am and out the door for my own training at 4:15am. I finish up training at 4:40am - my sessions typically last 20 - 25 minutes. So to keep my body fully charged, I turn out the lights at 8:30pm to get the right amount of sleep to function. This is one small step I have adopted that has enabled me to accomplish so much more throughout each day.

As the old saying goes, "Early to bed and early to rise makes a man healthy, wealthy and wise." There are a long list of health benefits that come from getting the right amount of sleep and rest that our bodies needs. The right amount of sleep and rest increases circulation, reduces stress, and speeds up our mental capacity. The biggest benefit of sleep is that it restores our energy. Our bodies are designed to repair themselves when we sleep. On a cellular level our body is hard at work when we sleep. Sleep allows our body to eliminate toxins at night while the body rests which is the primary way we actually detoxify our systems. If we limit our body's capacity to repair itself, we actually self-sabotage our ability to become a better version of ourselves. If we don't slow down and rest our body does not have enough time or opportunity to heal properly.

I recently challenged one of my workaholic clients in his sleep habits. He is your typical super-driven highly successful business person. He works hard and pushes his body to its limits with the secret motto of "I'll sleep when I'm dead" type of internal drive. I have been working with him for quite some time and he's committed himself to eat healthier and work out regularly. I have been coaching him to go to bed at the same time every night to acclimate his body to actually get the rest he needs. He fought me on this at first saying that even if he turns the light off he can't turn his mind off, but I have been diligent in pushing back. He has slowly adopted my advice overtime and is now showing up to the gym for his workouts more awake and alert. It is truly amazing how sleep can transform us, and one small change can makes such a huge impact.

## RECHARGE EXERCISE #2: Answer YES or NO to the following:

**Do you…**

1) **Eat Dinner Early?** _____ Eating late may leave undigested food in the stomach which interferes with our sleep patterns, and limits the blood flow to the rest of the body for cellular restoration.

2) **Avoid stimulants, particularly in the evening?** _____ Caffeine, sugar or any juices will interfere with the body's natural ability to relax, and also upsets the body's chemistry leading to interrupted sleep patterns.

3) **Reduce Mental Activity in the Evening?** _____ Allowing our minds to wind down and creating space from stress is essential in getting quality rest.

4) **Remove Technology from the Bedroom?** _____ Artificial stimulus often keeps us up at night, reengaging the mind. Light reading is better than late-night TV. Our beds were intended for sleep and sex.

5) **Avoid Exercise at Night?** _____ Exercise increases toxins in our muscles which interfere with our ability to fully rest during sleep. It is better to exercise in the

morning or during the day.

6) **Try to Avoid Alcohol Late at Night?** _____ Alcohol is a depressant and affects our body chemistry pulling blood to the stomach and liver which reduces our body's ability to naturally heal itself. It may help to 'unwind' and get to sleep faster, but once it metabolizes through our system (in about 2 hours or so) it interrupts our sleep patterns.

7) **Try to Go to Bed and Wake up at the Same Time Every Day?** _____ This requires discipline and effort, but over time reaps us the most rewards when it comes to getting a good night's rest.

## RECHARGE

*Self-awareness* is paramount when it comes to personally recharging. Understanding the types of activities and environments that are best suited for us to recharge our batteries are key components of living a healthy rhythm of life. National poling statistics estimate that 51 percent of Americans are extraverts, which means that the other 49 percent are introverts. According to the Meyer's Brigg Type Indicator, the major difference between extroverts and introverts is that extroverts tend to recharge during social situations while introverts do not. Extraverts are primarily recharged by their external environments and engaging in social activities. Introverts generally recharge by themselves and prefer their own company or that of a few close friends. This does not mean that extraverts are better socially and that introverts are shy, but that they have different preference for refueling emotionally, mentally and physically. Knowing which camp we fall into is important.

## EXTRAVERSION

These folks are recharged by activities and engaging events. Prefer to have a lot going on most of the time. Prefer working and playing in group settings. Rarely sit still, like to be active and are outgoing in new environments. Prefer to talk out ideas and problems. Put a check mark next to each bullet point that applies to you:

- I see myself as a people person and am outgoing
- I prefer to work in teams and groups with other people
- I have lots of different friends and people I see on a regular basis
- I get energized by new people, places, and things
- I react and then reflect

## INTROVERSION

These folks are recharged by focussing on their own inner world of ideas, pictures, memories and reflections. Prefer working alone or with one or two people at a time. Prefer to take time to reflect so that they have a clear idea of what is required of them before proceeding. Prefer to think through ideas and problems and then discuss. Put a check mark next to each bullet point that applies to you:

- I see myself as a reserved person and like to keep to myself
- I prefer to work by myself
- I have a few friends that I know really well
- I get energized by familiar people, places, and things
- I reflect before I react

When we understand how we prefer to recharge we are equipped with a clear template to see what additional activities we can say 'yes' to based on our other commitments. For extraverts, going out with the office on Thursday night after work can actually be an energy booster. For introverts, this is less appealing. Prioritizing our schedule becomes easier when we stop and ask ourselves if this activity is energy-giving or energy-depleting for us.

Introverts find it easier to recharge with familiar activities and interests. Most introverts enjoy reading, working on a hobby, exercising alone or one-on-one and different types of reflective activities like writing and reading. Studies have been conducted on introverted children that revealed when they were presented with an opportunity to participate in a group activity or game, they preferred to hang back and watch before they joined in. The researchers also discovered that even though the introverted children seemed to lack social engagement skills from the extroverted counterparts, their preference for engaging socially was simply different. They tended to listen more than they talked and were excellent listeners. This pattern of behavior holds true later in life as well. For us introverts, we should embrace who we are and how we're wired.

Extroverts find it easier to keep a lot of different plates spinning. Most extroverts enjoy team sports, exercising in social atmospheres, learning new hobbies and interests, and exploring different environments. In the study previously mentioned, researchers found that the extraverts preferred the following: They jumped right into new activities and were more vocal than their introverted counterparts. They tended to talk more and were excellent in participating in class discussion. Again, this pattern of behavior holds true later in life, and extraverts will serve themselves well by looking for active and stimulating environments that refuel them emotionally, mentally, and physically.

## PLUG IN, PULL AWAY

Figuring out how we recharge is paramount if we hope to live a healthy rhythm of life and achieve our goals. Understanding what activities give us energy and what activities deplete us of energy is crucial. With awareness comes clarity, and with clarity comes the ability to respond. Understanding our preference for recharging is key if we hope to finish what we start.

I am an introvert in an extraverted career. It is hard to find a quiet moment to fully recharge my batteries during the day. So I have adopted a morning ritual that energizes me throughout the day. I have discovered the activity and environment I need to create to recharge my energy. For me this means working out first thing in the morning. As an introvert, when I begin to feel run down, stressed or just looking for a jolt of energy, I need to recharge and refocus my body by spending some time in solitude. To me, there is no better time to do this than the pre-dawn hours before the city wakes up. There's just something about the quietness and stillness of the early morning hours that fill my tank of inspiration and give me the energy I need to become a better version of myself each day.

For the introverts out there who find themselves in extraverted jobs, it is essential that we adopt certain patterns of disconnecting from the masses in order to replenish the energy we have spent in our current roles. Weekends are sacred and down-time is essential. This comes into play for those of us who need alone time in order to engage our colleagues, families and friends in healthy ways. For those introverts who spend a lot of time investing in others, it is important to take some time to pull away and recharge. How we define 'down-time' is quite different than our extraverted counterparts.

For the extraverts out there it is equally important to identify what activities refuel and how to weave these events and opportunities into the everyday fabric of life. Extraverts also have limited amounts of energy to pull from, and it is essential that extraverts receive the proper amounts of connection and activity that replenishes their reserves. For example when working on projects or activities that require a lot of alone time, it is best if extroverts interject frequent breaks and process ideas collaboratively with a colleague.

The heart of the matter is in examining if we are operating in a healthy rhythm of life. This can be broken down into different parts:

- Are we running on fumes or tapping into an adequate source of energy?
- Are we getting the right amount of sleep at night or burning the candle at both ends?
- Are we eating the right foods at the right times throughout the day or still supplementing sleep by sugar- and caffeine-loading?
- Are we taking time for ourselves to actually pull away from the frantic fast-paced nature of the working world or going full-steam ahead?
- Are we aware of what activities refuel our batteries or still in the dark about what we need to do in order to reenergize?
- Are these activities a regular part of our weekly and monthly calendars or good ideas that we might get to someday?

A lot of us read these questions and immediately get hit with thoughts of guilt or anxiety. Guilt is about the past. It is a reaction to choices we have previously made that have brought us to the place we find ourselves at today. Anxiety is about the future. It is the worry of what might happen if we actually stopped. What if our plates stopped spinning or if we let a ball drop? We tell ourselves that we have to keep moving at this pace, and that we cannot afford to stop. Too many people are counting on us. We have too many responsibilities to just call a time-out. The truth is that we have to stop or at least slow down if we don't want to burn out.

Guilt and anxiety are different than conviction. Conviction literally means "with strong faith." When we make choices based on our convictions, we are living a purposeful life. When we make a choice to go to bed early, or say no to a late night snack, based on our convictions, we are choosing to not be a victim of the herd mentality. When we live by our convictions, we are able to decipher the difference between good, better and best. Guilt is a burden and anxiety is chaos, but conviction brings clarity. When we revisit our purpose and define our legacy we have a clear picture of the steps that it will take to achieve our goals.

## TIME

Time is a precious commodity. We can spend it, waste it or invest it. How we spend our time is a clear indicator of our values and what matters most to us. According to the US Census Bureau, the average life expectancy for an American is 78.2 years. That means that on average we get 78 Springs, Summers, Falls and Winters. This break down to roughly 28,562 days (including leap years) or 685,488 hours on average. The sobering reality is that all of us get 24 hours a day, and all we really have is today. Let's assume that we have adopted a healthy sleep schedule and are getting the recommended 8 hours of sleep a night. As previously mentioned Americans work an average of 45 hours in the office and 7 hours at home, or roughly 10.4 hours a day. Add in the average commute time of 52 minutes round trip and we're at roughly 11 hours a day spent in work-related activities.

Simple math factoring in sleeping (8 hours) and working (11 hours) leaves us with 5 hours. On average Americans spend an additional hour eating breakfast, lunch and dinner each day. So now we're down to 4 hours of leisure or "free" time, assuming we don't have kids to look after or take care of.

What are we doing with those 4 hours?

TV is not bad in and of itself, but is it best? Rarely do people come to the end of their life and say, "Man, I wish I would have spent more time watching Seinfeld reruns." What could we accomplish with those 4 hours each day? In his insightful book, Outliers, Malcolm Gladwell put forth the theory that individuals become "experts" in a particular field when they accumulate 10,000 hours in that area. If Gladwell is right, by the age of 8 our children are experts at watching TV. According to the A.C. Nielsen Co., the average American watches more than 4 hours of TV each day which equates to spending roughly 13 years of our life in front of the tube.

What could we do with 13 years of life? That's the same amount of time it takes to make it from kindergarten through graduation. At the end of our lives we have a diploma in advertising, soap operas and reality TV. For those of us in our 30s we could spend those remaining 6.5 years pursuing a hobby, writing a book, learning a new language, playing a sport, or volunteering. We could invest that time. Don't get me wrong, entertainment has its place, and sometimes it's easier to just roll home and let our favorite television programs wash over us…but is it the best?

## RECHARGE EXERCISE #3 – Answer the following questions:

**What do you *like* to do?**

**Do these activities help recharge your energy tank?**

## POWER NAP

A lot of parents put their children down for an afternoon nap on a regular basis. Some parents do this just out of a sheer desperation to have a bit of peace in the midst of chaotic childrearing, others do it because they know that their children need the rest. The truth is that we might all benefit from a mid-day siesta. Recent scientific research suggests that naps drastically enhance cognitive function. The research has shown that 20 to 30 minutes is best optimal recharging. This short time allows for only a light sleep that takes us into Stage Two of the sleep cycle, which increases our chance of quickly coming back into alertness. If we nap for more than 30 minutes we enter Stages Three and Four, reversing the effect of the "power nap." Simply put, naps make us more productive.

What do Leonardo da Vinci, Thomas Edison, and John F Kennedy have in common? They all took daily naps. Edison was almost religious in his devotion to pulling away from his creative endeavors to recharge. The man who invented the light bulb possibly could teach us a thing or two about recharging. According to a recent study done at the Mayo Clinic, researchers monitoring the brain activity of 15 napping individuals discovered that the right side of the brain (the hemisphere most associated with creativity) rapidly worked while the left side of the brain was at rest, basically concluding that napping makes us more creative and productive.

Some companies are experimenting with this theory allowing their employees to kick back and catch a quick nap to increase their productivity for the rest of the day. Google and Zappos.com are two companies that have caught on to the trend and even have designated space for their employees to crash out. These companies have seen the effects in their bottom lines as well rested employees are more engaged, more productive and more likely to work at optimal levels.

How much more productive could we be if we took a half hour to recharge each day? What would it look like if instead of reaching for an afternoon coffee or soda, we reached for the office light switch instead? For some of us this would not be acceptable behavior in the workplace, but for others it might be worth kicking back and closing our eyes for a half hour a day.

## PASSION

A common question that all of us have been asked upon first meeting folks is, *"What do you do?"* This question is okay, and we can formulate some type of response that gives people a picture of what our work life is and how we pay the bills. However, an even better question that cuts to the heart (literally) is, *"What do you like to do?"* That simple 4-letter addition taps into our souls. Honestly answering it can reveal the activities that actually recharge us and give us life.

*Maximizing our energy is all about identifying and engaging in activities that fill up our tank.* For some of us this is going on a long walk by ourselves, for others it's participating in a group or hanging out with family. Whatever it is that we *like* to do, incorporating that activity into our weekly rhythm of life is essential to becoming the best version of ourselves we can be.

Passion is the heart of the matter, and for the majority of folks out there it is so important to understand what it is that we're passionate about. Most of us don't have the luxury of getting paid for our passions, but all of us can invest an hour or two a week in an activity that gives us life. This is one of the healthiest things that we can do for ourselves, our employers, and our families. Studies show that when we spend even an hour a week engaged in a task or activity that we're passionate about, like volunteering or playing sports, our productivity in other areas of our life is positively affected. It seems counterintuitive to spend time on ourselves, but "me" time actually moves us to "we" time. It's an old school principle, but we cannot give what we do not have. We have to recharge, even if it's on the go.

Merriam-Webster defines passion as, "ardent affection that demands action" and, " an intense, driving, or overmastering feeling or conviction." Both of these definitions sum up what we're talking about in regards to passion. Whatever the activity or idea is that fires us up and moves us forward, it is worth exploring. Tapping into our passions unleashes fuel for the journey. When we are engaged in those activities we not only feel alive, we have more life to give and energy to extend to others.

## FINISHING WELL

When it comes to discovering purpose and leaving a legacy of significance and meaning for the next generation, maximizing our energy is at the core of the conversation. If discipline is doing the right thing the right way at the right time over and over again, our ability to finish well is dependent on living a healthy rhythm of life. Perseverance is about pressing through difficulty and overcoming disappointment. We have to be fighting for something bigger than ourselves, and we have to have staying power. We can only finish strong by understanding how we personally recharge, by getting the right amount of sleep at night, by engaging in activities that refuel us, and by slowing down. Regular pit stops are necessary if we want to operate at our best, refuel our tanks, and finish well.

# *Chapter Three:* RECHARGE: Maximizing Energy

*"Have courage for the great sorrows of life and patience for the small ones; and when you have laboriously accomplished your daily task, go to sleep in peace. God is awake."*  — Victor Hugo

## Week Three Reading Plan
### Reading / Reflection / Result

**Monday**
- Read Chapter Three

**Tuesday**
- How do you prefer to recharge?

**Wednesday**
- How can maximizing your energy help you achieve your Purpose?

**Thursday**
- Re-Read Chapter Three...

**Friday**
- What is your biggest obstacle to achieving your Purpose? Why?

**Saturday**
- What stood out to you the most from this chapter? Why?
- What are you going to do about it?

**Sunday**
- Rest

# CHAPTER FOUR:
## *PLAY: Infusing Joy*

*"Joy is the infallible sign of the presence of God."*
- Pierre Teilhard de Chardin

The wonderful thing about children is that they naturally know how to play and move. I have two little girls and the youngest one has just started crawling, rolling over, pulling up herself up, and squatting. What my youngest daughter is doing right now, in this developmental stage, is exactly what I am teaching my grown-up clients to do in the gym - how to squat, crawl, roll over and pull up. My other daughter is going through a silly exploration stage right now. Just last week I brought her up to the gym for her watch me work with a few clients. We have a few TRX suspension straps that hang down from a pull up bar. When she saw them for the first time, she just grabbed ahold of the handles and started to swing around. She was playfully exploring her environment. I even caught her doing pushups the other day, and we've never actually taught her to do them! Children intuitively know how to stay fit and healthy. They reactively explore movement through repeated trail and error. They were born with incredible mobility and learn to create stability by exploring movement. Perhaps above all, play is a simple joy that is a cherished part of childhood.

As children we saw exercise as play. As adults we see it as working out. Over the years we have forgotten how to move as we did as children. Irish playwright George Bernard Shaw stated it like this: "We don't stop playing because we grow old; we grow old because we stop playing." A lot of us lose the ability to do basic movement patterns - squat, crawl, climb, roll, skip, and jump. We forget how to move and end up losing our range of motion. Part of this can be attributed to aging, but most of it has to do with the fact that we live sedentary lifestyles. We have forgotten how to play.

A lot of us think back to our childhood when we hear the word "play." We reflect on recess, team sports and summer days spent riding bikes with friends. I personally think back on how much fun it was to be active as a kid, making up new games to play, climbing trees and exploring our limits on the jungle gym. My friends and I discovered roller hockey in the 7th grade. We spray painted our street to create a rink and hand crafted our goals out of PVC pipe and mesh netting. We played it until we got tired of it. Football, basketball, ping pong, soccer, hide-and-seek, tag...it didn't matter. We played for the sheer enjoyment of it, which liberated us from a sense of time ("Mom, I lost track of time!") and inspired a desire to continue ("Do we have to come in?"). What we didn't realize then was that we were seasonally changing our sports, our routines. This kept us in engaged, in great shape and injury free.

When we played as children we were growing physically, mentally, and emotionally. We were learning how to use our muscles. Through imitation we were developing balance and coordination. We were developing as little people and learning while kicking a ball, shooting a basket, swinging on a rope or climbing a tree. Through play we were discovering our own capacities and the world in which we lived. It almost seems too simple, but when we play we are at our core discovering what it is to be alive. Through play we mature from basic motor skills to fine motor skills. Recreational activities are just that, they "re-create" us when we engage in them.

There are a lot of physical benefits to playing. Playing boosts our immune system, lowers our blood pressure, and helps us develop strength and endurance. There are also relational benefits to playing. Studies show that playing improves our psychological mood and reduces the chance of depression in active children and adults. Playing is also linked to higher self-esteem and the ability for children and adults to socialize. Play can serve as a time to decompress, refocus and shift gears from the hurried and stressful lifestyle we live. The bottom line is that we are healthier, more socially balanced, and are more productive the more we play.

Play has had a huge impact on my own development. In the 3rd grade, I was diagnosed with dyslexia and struggled with very low self-esteem and confidence. On top of reading a number sequences out loud with a patch over one eye to help curve the dyslexia, I was assigned to read Joy Wilt Berry's book, *Handling Your Ups and Downs*. The book empowered children by helping them become responsible so they can have control over their lives that they want and need.

Since I was labeled in the classroom and had to spend evenings reading self-help books for kids, play became my outlet of freedom from the constraints that only held me back. I acted as if play was my job. Soon play became my catalyst towards boosting my confidence, self-esteem and ultimately, my happiness.

I love the way Phil Jackson talks about being present in his book, *Sacred Hoops*:

*In basketball - as in life - true joy comes from being fully present in each and every moment, not just when things are going your way. Of course, it's no accident that things are more likely to go your way when you stop worrying about whether you're going to win or lose and focus your full attention on what's happening right this moment.*

As I look back on the pick up games we played throughout the summers or before the first school bell rang before class, the focus was on the actual experience, not on accomplishing 60 minutes of play. It was a period of purposeful, fun and pleasurable time with my friends. I could stop worrying about the dyslexia and lack of self-confidence. I knew that when I was engaged in play, I was developing new skills that would build the resiliency I needed to face future challenges.

The new skills I developed - imagination, dexterity, courage, strength, persistence, discipline and leadership - eventually led me to the soccer field. Through team sports, such as soccer, we learn a lot about our identity and belonging. I look back on the experience of playing now and realize just how much I grew as a person from working hard to achieve a common goal with the same group of people. What made it so enjoyable was that we were a close-knit team going through all of the hard work of practices, along with the highs of winning and lows of losing. There's not anything quite like giving every ounce of mental, physical, and psychological energy in order to achieve the same goal. Soccer taught me the joy of community and the power of friendship. Team sports brought out the best in me because it demanded I be my best. It also developed my character and forced me to discover my leadership capabilities. I think back on the teams I played on and truly believe that we were successful on the field because we enjoyed each other off the field.

Maybe you've never played a team sport or competed in athletics, but undoubtedly we all remember our playground days. The impact of playing with others not only gives us instant accountability, but it engages a common need that all of us have as relational people. Life is designed to be lived in healthy, playful relationships with others. I experienced this through team sports, maybe you experienced this on a family vacation, at summer camp, or on a road trip in college. Undoubtedly, what made those experiences better was the fact that we weren't alone.

## PLAYTIME

According to recent research, play can have a direct impact on us in the areas of creativity, stress management and our overall physical health. For those of us who burn the candle at both ends in the office, playful physical activity reduces stress and increases productivity. Assisted living and long-term care facilities have discovered that regular play times help their patrons maintain clear thought, increase their short term memory and helps with overall morale. The benefit of engaging in physical activity increases our brain function, decreases our risk for disease and helps us stay socially active. No matter what stage in life we find ourselves in, we're never too old to play.

Gordon Sturrock, play-worker and theorist, describes play this way, "Play is a set of behaviors that are freely chosen, personally directed, and intrinsically motivated." If we think back to the playground at school or the games we played as children with our friends, all three of these characteristics were present. As adults we can become so structured – we think being fit requires a method or program but in reality we don't need a professional to watch over us. It really is child's play.

If we watch kids on a playground for 30 minutes we'd probably see them do a dozen different things. They will start and finish over and over again. They play and they move on...over and over. They learn to push as hard as they can and then recover. We could learn a lot about movement and activity from our kids at recess. In our driven achiever society we feel like we have to measure everything. Somehow we think that counting reps and watching the clock will make us thinner, faster and stronger and what ends up happening is that we lose the fun in playing. No wonder we call it "working out."

I have a client who was looking to add in some extra days of play to his routine outside of the gym. He knew that running any distance (the standard 3 mile "jog") was out of the question.

It was not the fact that he couldn't do it, but more that running miles bored him. It wasn't motivating to go out and pound the pavement.

We talked about different ways he could add conditioning into his weekly play time. What we came up with, I feel, was a complete game changer for those of us who do not like running long distances. My facility is located directly across the street from a school. On the school grounds are two sport fields - a baseball and softball field. The plan we came up with - run the bases!

It's hard to imagine, right? My clients' conditioning was literally rounding all the bases. Sometimes he would sprint to 1st base. At times, he would run out a double or stretch it to a triple. Then there was always the inside-the-park home run that completely left him gassed. He even ran the bases in the opposite direction to avoid an overuse injury from always turning the same way.

When he became bored of running the bases, he would venture over to the 6 row bleachers behind home plate. Again, this fit his "training personality." He liked short bursts of impact versus running longer distances. With the bleachers, he would run up the 6 steps and then back down. Repeat it a few times and then head back to the bases. He kept it interesting. He truly played each and every conditioning session which kept him motivated to stay consistent - the ultimate key to long-term success. His creative approach to working out gave him the personal incentive to reach his health and fitness goals

A simple formula for what my client discovered is: **Imagination + Perspiration = Inspiration**

I believe the primary reason we don't persevere when it comes to achieving our physical fitness goals is that we have lost the ability to play. In fact, most of us take ourselves too seriously. Don't get me wrong, we should be committed and have a plan to become a better version of ourselves, but living a life of purpose is about enjoying life as much as it is about leaving a meaningful mark on history. F U N are the first letters in funeral, and if we're not careful about adopting a playful attitude when it comes to physical activity as adults, we'll definitely head to an early grave. I don't know very many young people who started out in life wanting to grow old and bitter. Leaving a meaningful legacy includes joy and laughter.

## LAUGHTER IS GOOD FOR THE SOUL

Movement is essential to life. Perhaps above all, play is a simple joy that is a cherished part of childhood. Then adult responsibilities ensued and we stopped. "The whole culture is suffering from over-conscious intentionality, over-seriousness, overemphasis on productivity and work," psychologist and cultural explorer Bradford Keeney said. "We've forgotten that the whole picture requires a dance between leisure and work." Now we are expected to move more. There in turn lies a major problem: We hate to workout. Dragging ourselves to the gym, trudging on the treadmills and banging the dumbbells around is repetitive and predictable. Is it any wonder why we view exercising like work?

We think we are not supposed to play as adults. We are supposed to have problems, be too busy, and have 'important' things to do. But as it turns out, there are few things more important to our joy and happiness in life than frequent doses of play. As a study led by Princeton researcher Alan Krueger found, of all the things on the planet, we're at our happiest when we're involved in engaging playful activities. Why not do more of that?

Engaged play allows us to tap into our true self, not the performance identity of the job we hold or the mask we display to others. Play relieves us of the burden to be someone we are not.

There's nothing on the line; it's just play. And when we are able to be our true selves, it's a huge stress buffer, reducing strain and burnout, boosting our immune system and pumping up vitality and energy, relieves

Infusing joy into our everyday life is essential if we want to do more than cross the finish line. The quality of the journey is as important as the destination. Laughter and joy fill up our emotional tank so that we can press through the difficult barriers in our health and fitness goals.

## MIXING IT UP

In order to achieve our health and fitness goals we have to change our mentality of viewing exercise as a "work out" by returning to the spontaneity and imagination of our childhood. Again this is a simple principle that if applied can bring amazing results. For some of us working out is serious business, but what if we could have serious fun and achieve our health and fitness goals? What if we simply approached exercise like we did when we were kids? What if we mixed it up?

At some point along the way, we have preferred the same workout routine - always running 3 miles, attending the same workout class, or, not doing anything at all (that is a routine as well!). We can get in to a rut by doing the same workout over and over again. We will never get different results the same old way. By changing things up and introducing some new life to our weekly exercise routine we can drastically improve our mentality when it comes to health and fitness. The changes we introduce don't have to be massive, but rather small steps taken daily.

I have a confession to make: I like to rollerblade. I discovered my affinity for rollerblading playing roller hockey in the street as kids. I have been rollerblading ever since. A few years back my wife, Cassie, got me a new pair. I know what you're thinking, how can this professional trainer be hooked on a passing fad? The truth, I just enjoy them. For me, rollerblading is a change of pace once a week. It's a chance for me to add some variety into my conditioning that brings a strong sense of play back to my routine. I love how Plato stated it: "Life must be lived as play."

When we incorporate different types of play from our childhood into our weekly routines, we can make our workouts fun and overcome the boredom and repetition of the same old routines. As physician George Sheehan said: "A man's exercise must be play, or it will do him little good." This may sound too simple or easy, but it works.

We should allow our training schedule to shift focus like Mother Earths routine of changing seasons. As the seasons change, we experience the true wonders of growth, opportunity, labor, and rest. When we mix things up, we even out the wear and tear on our bodies. We also stay fresh, beat boredom, and shock our muscles to adapt to the new routines. In essence, we have to change to grow.

If we fail to mix things up, overtraining and overuse will limit our pursuit. Instead of making progress from the constant and frantic exercise routine, we end up limiting our progress due to a lack of rest that our body needs. Most of the injuries that we pick up are from overuse, especially for the weekend warriors, long distance runners and those who push their limits every session. Doctors are making a lot of money off of folks that kill themselves doing the same type of exercise over and over again. And it isn't until we suffer a set back, forced to miss our routine, do we begin to notice and appreciate the benefits of change. When we mix it up and switch our routines, we add variety, stay mentally sharp, overcome workout plateaus and are more likely to avoid injuries.

## PLAY EXERCISE #1 – 5 Ways to take the "Work" out of Working Out

### *#1 Introduce a Sport you enjoy to your weekly routine...*

You don't have to be in a gym to get a good workout. You can swim, dance, play basketball, or go for a hike. Variety is the seasoning of life and it keeps us on our toes, literally, when it comes to our health and fitness routines.

### *#2 Take a different route to work...*

Only in America do four employees who live in the same neighborhood get into four SUVs and drive to the same location. Put down the car keys and grab your bike helmet. Choose to bike into work a couple of days a week instead of your normal commute. You'll reduce your carbon footprint and increase your exercise.

### *#3 Incorporate exercise into your daily life...*

Take a break from the big office meals, and pack a lunch for a small walk to a park near by the office. Take the stairs instead of the elevator. Walk after dinner. Join the local Y or office gym and workout instead of eating out. You'll look and feel better and have more energy throughout the day.

### *#4 Find a partner in crime...*

All of us need accountability and if you find a like-minded workout partner you have a better chance of achieving your goals. Both of you can motivate each other, cheer each other on, and encourage each other when you don't want to suit up and get your sweat on.

### *#5 Go back to grade school...*

Literally, go to the local school playground and utilize the equipment there. Use the monkey bars to do pull ups or just try to make it all the way across without putting your feet down.

The swings are a great tool for core exercises. Then just bear crawl your way through the open grass - forwards, backwards, and side to side. Just make sure school is not in session. It would be a little awkward for you to be playing during recess.

## THE HAPPINESS FACTOR

Playing makes us feel better. We can instantly see the impact of being in good shape; we're less winded and have more energy to face the day. When it comes to our brain and mood though, the connection isn't so clear.

In simple terms, when we start playing more, our brain recognizes this as a moment of stress, our heart pressure increases, and our brain thinks we are in a state of fight or flight. To protect itself from stress, our brains release a protein called BDNF (Brain-Derived Neurotrophic Factor). BDNF has a protective and also reparative element for our memory neurons and acts as a reset switch. That's why we often *feel* so at ease and things are clear after playing. We actually feel happiness. At the same time, endorphins, another chemical to fight stress, are released in our brain. The main purpose of our endorphins being released in our brains is to minimize the negative effects of exercise by blocking the feeling of pain and fatigue.

Needless to say, there is a lot going on inside our brain when we work out, but the effects feel great. New York Times best-selling author, Gretchen Reynolds, has written a whole book about happiness and the brain titled, *The First 20 Minutes*. Reynolds argues that in order to get the highest level of happiness and benefits for health, we do not have to become a professional athlete. In fact, the opposite is true; a much smaller amount of exercise is needed to reach the level where happiness and productivity in every day life peaks. She writes, "The first 20 minutes of moving around...provide most of the health benefits. We get prolonged life, reduced disease risk — all of those things come in in the first 20 minutes of being active…On exercise days, people's mood significantly improved after exercising. Mood stayed about the same on days they didn't, with the exception of people's sense of calm which deteriorated." All we have to do is get a focused 20 minutes of play in to get the full happiness boost every day.

## TRANSFORMATION

Happiness is not just a chemical release in our brain. True happiness is about discovering meaning in the mundane. True happiness isn't easily achieved. True happiness is intrinsically linked to the things that don't spoil or fade. True happiness is about discovering joy in our everyday life. Becoming a better version of ourselves is not just about physical health, it's as much about our emotional and mental well-being. When we clarify our purpose and work with dedicated passion to achieve our goals, we will undoubtedly change internally as well as externally. When we reach our health and fitness goals we gain confidence, a greater self-respect and have the strength and ability to be the person we have longed to be.

They say that beauty is skin deep, but the inverse is actually true. Beauty comes from the inside out. When we take the necessary steps to become a better version of ourselves we undoubtedly undertake an internal transformation as well. The result of the journey towards health and fitness is just as much about getting our mind and hearts set right. We not only look better, we genuinely feel better as well. When we talk about health and fitness we're talking about the tension between aligning our inner values with our outer abilities. We don't have to pursue extremes when it comes to getting our inner world to match our outer world. We just need to be aware that they're connected.

In a recent study conducted by a group of researchers from

Canada and the US, it was discovered that even modest amounts of weekly playtime boosted mental health of adolescents. The research showed that 3 hours of weekly physical activity helped the participants, "… with issues such as body dissatisfaction, social alienation and low self-esteem." When we start taking the necessary steps to achieve our health and fitness goals, there's something deeper going on. Change is inevitable when attached to a deeper purpose and a playful mindset.

## INFUSING JOY

Joy is defined by Merriam Webster as, "…the emotion evoked by well-being, success, or good fortune or by the prospect of possessing what one desires." When we say we need to play more we're getting at the heart of this definition, almost. Infusing joy is about more than an emotion evoked, however it is about possessing what we desire, especially when it comes to achieving our health and fitness goals. When we discover our purpose, set simple goals, and work hard to achieve them we have to infuse joy along the way if we don't want to burn out. Infusing joy is about not taking ourselves too seriously. Infusing joy is about working hard and playing hard. Infusing joy is about laughing out loud with people who are on the journey with us. Infusing joy is about having some serious fun as we become a better version of ourselves.

## *Chapter Four:* PLAY: Infusing Joy

*"Don't cry because it's over, smile because it happened."*
— Dr. Seuss

## <u>Week Four Reading Plan</u>
### Reading / Reflection / Result

**Monday**
- Read Chapter Four

**Tuesday**
- Do you incorporate play in your everyday life? Why or why not?

**Wednesday**
- How can infusing joy help you achieve your Purpose?

**Thursday**
- Re-Read Chapter Four...

**Friday**
- What is your biggest obstacle to achieving your Purpose? Why?

**Saturday**
- What stood out to you the most from this chapter? Why?
- What are you going to do about it?

**Sunday**
- Rest

# CHAPTER FIVE:
## *ORGANIZE:*
### *Embracing Responsibility*

*"The world is not to be put in order. The world is order. It is for us to put ourselves in unison with this order."*
                                                  - Henry Miller

One of the biggest indicators of whether or not we are going to be successful in achieving our purpose is our ability to take action and sustain that action day after day. Implementation is the key to becoming a better version of ourselves. We are all wired differently, so it is important that we understand our preference for organizing life. Some of us are detailed oriented down to the most minute detail, while others of us prefer to take life one day at a time and roll with the punches. The split in America is roughly 50/50. Half of us prefer to plan ahead, the other half like to move ahead and then plan. If "ready, fire, aim" is your motto you fall in the later half. If you prefer to make checklists for your checklists then you are in good company.

The thing to remember here is to not to beat ourselves up for what we're not, but to fully embrace how we are wired. This flies in the face of the American education system where we tend to focus on our weaknesses and work on being well-rounded. This is a lie minted in hell. We can spend the rest of our lives focusing on our weaknesses and getting nowhere, or we can embrace them and leverage our strengths and begin the journey of living out a purposeful life of meaning and impact. The starting place is realizing that we cannot be anyone else, and if we're not careful we will go mad trying to be someone we're not. We can only become a better version of ourselves by understanding who we are. When we do this we have taken the first step towards achieving the purpose we were put here on earth for. With clarity comes freedom and the ability to act on who we are in natural ways.

Without painting extremes, those who fall into the "Planner" category:

- Focus on the details in advance before taking action
- Focus on the task at hand and break it down into measurable parts
- Fear deadlines and work well ahead of them
- Naturally embrace and utilize goals, dates and routines to manage everyday life

And, those in the "Explorer" category:

- Prefer to plan on the go, and improvise in the moment
- Experiment with various ways of achieving goals and prefer to multi-task
- Acknowledge deadlines, but see them as elastic and malleable
- Fear commitments, prefer to explore possibilities and treat each day as an adventure

A lot of us will read the above characteristics and be confused, because we can tick a couple of those bullet points off in each category. For our purposes here and for the sake of clarity, we are all on a spectrum. I am a Planner, but my wife is an uber-Planner. Having an organized wife is such a blessing. My fault is my day-to-day taking care of the little details. I see things very big, and

Cassie sees the details. She's rock solid with the day-to-day. I've realized that I could accomplish these little details, but they are things that she enjoys and that Cassie is great at it. I have the great idea and know the necessary steps and Cassie walks beside me and helps implements them. She's able to take the things that I see and puts it in perspective and reality. My ability to "connect the dots" and her ability to cross the 't's and dot the 'i's' is a beautiful working relationship.

Benjamin Franklin was a Planner. He is famous for chunking time to experiment, work, eat and sleep. Here's an entry from his daily schedule:

- *Morning*: *The Question: What good shall I do this day?*
- *5:00am-8:00am:* *Rise, wash, and address Powerful Goodness! Contrive day's business, and take the resolution of the day; prosecute the present study, and breakfast*
- *8:00am-12:00pm:* *Work*
- *12:00pm-2:00pm:* *Read or look over my accounts and dine.*
- *2:00pm-6:00pm:* *Work*
- *6:00pm-10:00pm:* *Put things in their places. Supper. Music or diversion, or conversation. Examination of the day.*
- *Evening:* *The Question: What good have I done today?*
- *10:00pm-5:00am:* *Sleep*

I love that he started and ended the day with the same question, "What good shall I do this day?" and, "What good have I done today?" This is about as purposeful as it gets. He lived an ordered life and went down in history as a great achiever. He discovered and intentionally applied a daily discipline with a routine that worked for him. This is key for those of us who are Planners. It's good to map it out and pace ourselves to accomplish our goals for the day. Explorers might see this and think, "That's too religious of a schedule." This may not work for everybody, but for those who need to have things mapped out it is necessary for success. With clarity comes change, and with change comes progress.

Another part of my routine is that after I've gone through the mental prep for the day, I get my workout in. If I don't get my 'play' time in, my day feels a bit off and I'm a little crabby. I have to move and get the blood flowing if I hope to be focused throughout the day. It is just part of my daily routine. I don't have to kill it for an hour, 20-30 minutes will do. Some days I don't even break a sweat, but mentally I know that I need to move. My day is typically packed with client meetings, employee conversations, and other unforeseen issues that come with running my own business. Taking care of myself first is a priority, and getting a training in sets me on a good path for the day.

In our quest to become a better version of ourselves, we must follow an old airline safety announcement and "secure our own oxygen mask first." Before we can help others, we must first take care of ourselves. Before we can be solid leaders, we must first be healthy enough to show up everyday. Before we can bless our children with better upbringings and lives than we experienced, we must first role model what it means to live fit and healthy. Before we can lose fat, we must first be confident in ourselves enough to not "give-in" to peer pressure.

When we fail to maintain proper priorities, disappointment always results. We need to remember the 80/20 Principle: With the right priorities, 20% of our effort will get us 80% of the desired results. But with the wrong priorities, 80% of our effort will get us 20% of the desired results. It's not about working harder, but smarter. By securing our own oxygen masks first we have the ability to then help others do the same.

## STARTING AND FINISHING THE RIGHT WAY

Every morning before I even get out of bed I go through the routine of being thankful. This might take a few moments, but I start everyday with a brief prayer of gratitude.

"Grateful" defined:
*appreciative of the benefits received; expressing gratitude.*

Sometimes it takes a special day of "Giving Thanks' to remind us that we should be truly thankful for all the blessings we have. Of which, I 1,000% believe we should 'express gratitude' for our health each and every day.

Maybe it's because I deal with health & fitness on a daily basis. Maybe it's because I fully understand that we cannot accomplish our purpose in life if we don't have good health. Maybe it's because I know we can't give 100% of ourselves to helping others succeed if we're not 100% healthy. Maybe it's because I think about my life as an 80 year old: Do I want to have to be taken care of daily because of poor health? Do I want my family and loved ones to sacrifice their lives to take care of me because I neglected living fit and healthy? Or do I want live out my days here on this earth full of the energy needed to leave a lasting legacy?

We have a tendency to take our health for granted because the deterioration of it is such a slow and invisible process. Like a sinking ship, a small leak takes a while to cause its damage. But after a while, the leak becomes a rushing river. And then – BAM! – our seemingly good health is gone. Life takes an interesting and an unplanned turn – usually not in the direction we would like it to go.

An attitude of gratitude is not a miracle cure for poor health, but it does help us begin the process of truly appreciating how blessed we are. Giving thanks starts with one small step. A "Gratitude List" works like this:

Before our feet even hit the floor in the AM, we can mentally acknowledge one thing we're grateful for in life. This could be be a great nights sleep, our spouse, kids, a warm bed, roof over our head, a job, a special friend, etc.

Before we fall asleep at night, again we mentally acknowledge one small thing we're grateful for from our day. It could be that we landed a deal, watched our kids play outside, it could be a tough workout we completed, or it could be that comfy bed we're laying in.

As we begin to express our gratitude, we begin to acknowledge and see the positive things around us. If we kept up this attitude of gratitude for 365 days over the next year, then we would have over 730 experiences with friends and family to be truly thankful for…One day at a time.

## ORGANIZE EXERCISE #1: Gratitude List

**Personally I am grateful for…**

**Relationally I am grateful for…**

**Spiritually I am grateful for…**

**Professionally I am grateful for…**

## STARTING RIGHT

I have to get my mind right. Once my mind is engaged I ask myself, "What are the top 3 priorities for my day?" For me, these priorities can be broad or specific: Connecting relationally with my wife and my team; reading and researching a new project;

connecting with my clients. I try to put the big items on my mental map. I firmly believe in starting my day with a plan and working that plan throughout the day. This process is very simple, but effective.

I have a good friend who is on the opposite end of the spectrum. He would definitely fall into the "go with the flow" camp. He's been successful by learning how to leverage his affinity for bumping up against deadlines. He prefers to discover each day as it comes, but he also has developed systems that fit how he's wired. When he gets an appointment or schedules a meeting he automatically plugs it into his phone, and then moves onto the next item in his day. He plugs it in so he won't forget or lose it. When he rolls out of bed in the morning he looks at the day ahead and sees what his appointments are, which ones he needs to prepare for, and sporadically throughout the day comes back to the calendar. For him it's a catchall that he can reference so that he's in the right place at the right time. On the weekends, he rarely schedules anything thing in his calendar. This allows him the freedom to be creative and explore whatever might be hitting him at the moment. He's discovered a system that works for him.

What's key for explorers is the need to "feel/think" that they have options. In order to achieve goals, it's important for them to track the "big picture" items and flow throughout the day. An old piece of wisdom for this bunch, is to write down 2-3 things that must be done today, or this week somewhere visually where they can come back to it. A whiteboard is a great place to start, but it must be in a space that they can reference often throughout the week. Here are a couple of great app resources that are available for smart phones:

Evernote, www.evernote.com
Simple Note, www.simplenoteapp.com
Springpad, www.springpad.com

These are all great tools that Explorers and Planners can both utilize to stay focused on the task at hand. The bottom line is to discover a system that works for you and work that system daily.

## SPINNING PLATES

As we stated in chapter one, when we fail to plan we plan to fail. It doesn't matter whether we live by a detailed checklist or like to roll with the punches, we have to step back and take a look at what really matters most to us. Simply asking ourselves, "Which plates can stop spinning?" could be the healthiest way to getting a grip on what is essential for us to be successful in life, especially when it comes to our personal health and fitness goals. When we start with our purpose for our plan, the way forward becomes clear. When we identify what we're fighting for and why it is important, our goals and next steps rise above the fray and chaos of everyday life.

There are lots of contributing factors to why we tend to over-commit and under-deliver. The number one reason we get pulled away from accomplishing our purpose and sticking with our plans is that we have an inability to say no. Planners and Explorers, alike, struggle with this obstacle. We naturally feel called to help people and end up getting pulled in a million different directions throughout the day. We need to remember that we have limited resources. There is only so much time and energy to use each day. We have to revisit our purpose and learn to set boundaries and recognize our limits on a daily basis. Faithfulness to what matters most will ultimately enable us to help more people over the long haul. Daily faithfulness to our purpose is a catalyst for helping others, because we will stay focused and organized to what matters most and in turn help others set healthy boundaries and take responsibility for their own lives.

Another simple principle we can apply to live a more organized life is to schedule time to think strategically about our daily goals. So many folks shoot from the hip and live reactively to life, rather than proactively. If you're a Planner it's a bit more natural to think first and then act, but for Explorers this is a less natural process. Both types can benefit from setting aside time to think. Strategy is all about thinking through the next few moves. For Planners it may be helpful to write everything out and flesh out every detail on a regular basis. For Explorers it's probably easier to think through the top 3 things that they may need to do tomorrow in light of what they experienced today. Again, we need to use our purpose statement as a filter to determine what is essential and what is periphery to being successful. A good pattern to adopt a rhythm of strategic thinking is to divert daily, withdraw weekly and meditate monthly.

As we discussed in chapter three, we also need to learn how to slow down. When this becomes a part of our weekly rhythm of life we gain perspective on what the next right move is for us to be successful. Too many of us move at an insane pace and are addicted to activity. We end up becoming addicted to chaos and rarely stop long enough to focus on what is essential in order to stay organized. Again, when we slow down we are actually being counter-cultural. In a nation addicted to more, faster, and busyness, making a conscious choice to go against the flow stands out. I am not advocating laziness, but intentionality shifting gears in what we invest our time and resources in. By slowing down we gain the perspective to see if we're living purposeful lives.

One of the biggest gifts we can give ourselves when it comes to living an organized life is to simplify. As we've already discussed throughout the book, simple is best. We have a hard time believing this because we love to complicate life. Simplicity is not a lack of sophistication, in fact, it is sometimes more difficult to break things down into their most basic terms. But, when we do take the time to cut to the core of what is essential, when we cut through the clutter we free ourselves to spend our time, energy and money on what matters most. Organization is all about arranging and ordering life. A simple system is an effective system. When we start with our purpose as our foundation for making decisions, all of a sudden the right choices become quite clear. Armed with a clear purpose we can easily determine what we need to do next, regardless of whether we prefer a checklist or a parachute.

## SIMPLE TIPS FOR ORGANIZING

### ASSESS

We need to take stock of life right now. Do we have simple goals that make sense in light of our Purpose? Are we making progress in accomplishing these? Are they too complicated for us to gain momentum and traction in accomplishing them? Reviewing our goals regularly can help give us the clarity and confidence we need to take the next step. We should be writing these down and reviewing them regularly. Assessing is all about testing ourselves and taking a hard look at our choices. Are our choices moving us towards becoming a better version of ourselves? If not, we need to reprioritize and take the next step.

### DECLUTTER

Chances are we still may have too much going on in order to devote the right time, energy and resources into our heath and fitness goals. Which plates can stop spinning right now? What tasks can we either delegate or give away in order to keep the main thing the main thing and accomplish our Purpose? Decluttering our lives is all about pruning the unnecessary tasks and commitments that are not giving us a return on the investment of our time, energy and resources. Learning to let go is hard, but necessary if we are going to trim the fat from our schedules and our waistlines.

## ARRANGE

Arranging our lives is all about putting the right things in the right places at the right times. This means understanding our boundaries and setting healthy deadlines for accomplishing our health and fitness goals in order to become a better version of our selves. We can arrange our schedules, our meals, our work-outs, our commitments, our time, and our budgets so that they align with our Purpose. This takes intentionality and honesty, but when we consciously choose to take responsibility for our lives we become mature adults able to discern what the difference between good, better, and best. Why would we settle for a chaotic existence when we can simplify and live an organized life that helps us and others?

## REVISIT

Go back to the beginning. Literally. When we revisit why we began this journey in the first place we gain clarity and reassurance for the arduous journey ahead. This means trusting ourselves and the end result we hope to accomplish. By revisiting our Purpose and goals regularly we gain the confidence to forge ahead and pay the price for an uncommon life. By revisiting our simple plan we maintain a healthy rhythm of life that affords us the best opportunity to become the people we long to be. When we revisit the old version of ourselves we gain passion for moving forward. This may be painful, but it is purposeful.

## LESS IS MORE

We have all heard it before, but less really is more. Sounds counterintuitive and countercultural, but that does not mean it is not true. The simple fact is that so many of us have so much stuff, so many commitments, and so much going on that we have lost any real sense of who we are and what we're about. One of the main goals of this chapter and major themes of this book is the rediscovering of what matters most. I truly believe that all of us were created for a purpose greater than ourselves. I have tried to build my life and my business on this timeless truth that less is more. I have sacrificed and gone without so that I could accomplish more. Time and time again this has paid off. I would choose to be David any day of the week against the Goliath's of this world.

I am an organized guy. I live a disciplined life. This discipline is built around old-school wisdom that I learned from my parents who learned it from their parents. Simplicity is the art of getting the most out of what you have on hand and accomplishing more with less. So many folks have bought into the opposite of this and have found that they are actually accomplishing less with more. We do not need more fitness programs, or more diet programs, or more of the crap that the world is selling; what we really need is to simplify our lives and take responsibility for what we already have been given. The life we long for is not someone else's, but our own. We have the necessary tools, knowledge and experience already within us if we would simply stop long enough to take a deep and honest look at our own hearts. Understanding our Purpose is not rocket science, but it is heart surgery.

We need to slow down long enough to take stock of what really matters. When we do this we gain the clarity and insight to understand what we actually want to live for and accomplish. With these goals in hand we can create a simple plan that we can put to work. Some of us are hyper-organized and others of us are shooting from the hip. Both can work if we understand what our target is and make sure we're aiming in the right direction. Organizing is all about prioritizing, which is all about clarifying between what is worth our time, energy, and resources and what isn't. The most important thing we do in life is make choices. Those choices can lead us towards chaos or towards order. So many of us choose chaos when simple reflection on our past would reveal what actually is wise for us to do next.

Less really is more, when it comes to life. Every day roughly 6,700 people in the US die. The reality is that so many more stopped living a long time ago because they lacked the self-control and self-awareness to choose life. There is a narrow road that leads to life, but very few people find it. I want to be one of the few who do. It's not popular to swim upstream or go against popular thinking, but I don't want to be popular…I want to live a life of purpose. The "more" I have discovered by choosing to be content with the "less" far surpasses the junk the world is selling for $19.99 on infomercials. We can't buy happiness, but we can discover the gift of a disciplined and prudent life. It's not sexy, but it is good, beautiful, and true. Less is really more.

## EMBRACING REALITY

If we are deeply honest with ourselves about our ability or inability to live an organized and disciplined life we will have taken the first and most important step towards embracing reality. For Planners, it may be hard to let go of those tasks and commitments that are holding us back from focusing on what matters most. This means letting go of our need to control everything and zeroing in on the essentials of life. For Explorers, it may be quite difficult to see the trees for the forest. Slowing down long enough to identify the targets we're shooting from the hip at will increase our likelihood of success. In both cases this means embracing how we're wired and leveraging our strengths, refining our skills, and increasing our knowledge to be the best we can be in order to live a disciplined and simplified life.

Our ability to live an organized life is directly related to our ability to come to grips with who we are and how we prefer to structure the daily details life throws at us. When we understand our preference for Planning and Exploring we are light years ahead of the masses that stumble and speed ahead without the clarity and self-awareness of discovering a life of Purpose. By going 'old-school' and keeping it simple we cannot help but accomplish more.

# *Chapter Five:* ORGANIZE: Embracing Responsibility

*"The price of greatness is responsibility."*
— Winston Churchill

## <u>Week Five Reading Plan</u>
### Reading / Reflection / Result

**Monday**
- Read Chapter Five

**Tuesday**
- What type of organizer are you?

**Wednesday**
- How can embracing your preference for organizing help you achieve your Purpose?

**Thursday**
- Re-Read Chapter Five…

**Friday**
- What is your biggest obstacle to achieving your Purpose? Why?

**Saturday**
- What stood out to you the most from this chapter? Why?
- What are you going to do about it?

**Sunday**
- Rest

# CHAPTER SIX:
## *SEEK:*
## *LEVERAGING ACCOUNTABILITY*

*"We spend a life owning stuff and trying to acquire more stuff. Yet we do so little owning our own actions and decisions in life. Hence we hold our self to very little if any accountability to the kind of life we wish we would live."* — Brandon A. Trean

Roughly 45 million people own a membership to their local gym. Of those 45 million, only 33% use their membership. 30 million people last year wasted close to 12.7 billion dollars on good intentions. But like the saying goes, "Hell is paved with good intentions." The reason most people fail is because they try to go it alone. We will constantly lie to ourselves about our good intentions if we try to live without accountability. Healthy accountability and expertise is a catalyst for real results and lasting change.

Accountability works because it is much easier to lie to ourselves than it is to lie to others. When other people are counting on us to show up, we are less likely to choose the path of least resistance. When other people are expecting us to follow through, we are less likely to drop the ball and quit. When other people are there to support us and challenge us, we are more likely to persevere and finish the race.

Accountability is as simple as letting someone else know about a goal we have and asking them to check up on us. It doesn't matter whether it is a person, a group, a trainer or a coach. What matters is that we are honest about the goals we're pursuing and we give that person, group, trainer or coach permission to hold us accountable. If we really want to change and grow as human beings, then there's got to be some type of real consequence. If we want to become a better version of ourselves, then there is a price to be paid.

There are two types of people out there when it comes to learning life's toughest lessons: those that can learn from the successes and failures of others; and those that learn best through experiencing the success and failure themselves. The truth is that it is not a tragedy to experience failure in this life; but the real tragedy is to experience failure and not learn from it. Experience can definitely be life's greatest teacher. For those of us that learn the hard way, dealing with failure is a natural part of the human experience. How we respond to disappointment and failure shapes our future and can either propel us towards becoming a better version of ourselves, or block us from accomplishing our best. Most of us need the help of others if we're going to change.

I am a professional fitness trainer by trade, and most of my clients pay me to be their accountability partner when it comes to their health and fitness goals. Over time, I become a small quiet voice in their head: "You're packing your training shoes right? I've been to countless hotels that do and do not have a gym. You can train when you're on the road." I've had quite a few of my clients take pictures of their meals and text them to me on the spot. One client came clean and told me that there were times when he wanted to take pictures and push the chips and diet coke out of the frame, but he knew that he needed to be honest if he hoped to change and grow.

For me, accountability is not a one size fits all approach. We are all wired differently. Some folks need me to press them daily, others just need to check in. I'm not a big stickler to weighing people, but every now and then it's good to check in and see where they stand. Figuring out what the client needs for that particular season of life is paramount to not injuring their spirit or deterring them from accomplishing their health and fitness goals.

I've recently been working with one of my clients to help them quit smoking. The first thing I did was figure out the pattern of when and where they smoked. We figured out that it mostly revolved around transitional times to and from work. Every morning this client would stop and have a cup of coffee and a smoke. We decided to change up their routine to break the habit. We rerouted their drive to work and sent them on the course of getting a smoothie. A small ½ a mile difference set them up for success. On the front end of our relationship, I was asking them about their smoking every single day for 60 days. Then I eased off. Eventually they quit.

Life happens, and my client had a rough patch and went back to smoking. So this time around I had them call me every time before they were going to smoke a cigarette. I did not try to talk him out of it, I just wanted him to take responsibility for his actions. This is exactly the type of accountability that this specific client needed. Now the client is training to compete in a race, a purpose that has empowered them to make better choices. With my accountability, this is something that we're working on together...one day at a time.

In my own journey, my wife, Cassie, has been the greatest voice of accountability. She knows me better than anybody else. She knows if I need to speak with my coach, or ring up my best friend. She knows when to push me in the right direction. I'm selfish at times when it comes to scheduling work and our family time. When I'm not living out my values she calls me on it. When outside events affect us as a family she calls me out. I try very hard to receive it. Both her and my best-friend have permission to call me out and help me to become a better version of myself. They have a very direct approach with me. After I have time to process the truth they are speaking in my life I eventually come around and accept it. At first I want to justify my actions, but I eventually accept their help and use it to grow.

Healthy accountability is not always fun, but it is always good.

## THE ABILITY TO RESPOND

Accountability is powerful when it enables and empowers us to take personal responsibility for our Purpose, our goals, our passion, our everyday lives. Author Stephen Covey says, "Accountability is response-ability." All of us have heard it before, but it really is true that the only thing standing in the way of us accomplishing our best in life is ourselves. It's our own inability to take responsibility for our life. This requires that we stop playing the blame game.

Merriam-Webster defines blame as, "to place responsibility on another." Maturity is about letting go of our past, embracing our present, and leveraging our future. The rite of passage into adulthood means coming face to face with the reality that we are the only person that can determine the quality of our lives. Excuses are dead weight that will drown our future. We cannot afford to carry the baggage of our past if we want to experience the freedom our best futures hold. Isn't it time we stop blaming others and start enlisting them in helping us create the life we long to live?

"We cannot escape the responsibility of tomorrow by evading it today," thoughts on living with integrity from honest Abe. The present is all we have. If we do the right things today, no matter how minute or how small, tomorrow will take care of itself. As the saying goes, everyday has enough trouble of its own. Right thinking is half the battle; right living moves us from good ideas to actual living better. Taking responsibility for our lives is about acting on the truth we know about ourselves and living in response to that truth in the moment.

We accomplish our goals when we do the next right thing, take the next step, choose the next healthy option, and seek the right accountability. Becoming a better version of ourselves is not an isolated event. Becoming a better version of ourselves is a determination to do all the small things well. Helen Keller said it this way, "I long to accomplish a great and noble task, but it is my chief duty to accomplish small tasks as if they were great and noble."

Accountability is really about discipline and consistency. It's so easy to do and so easy not to do. When we see someone who takes the time and has the self-discipline to do the small things, we find someone who is successful in life. A simple example of this is having the self-disciple to wake up at the same time every day. This affords us the opportunity to keep the rhythm of life moving whether we're at home or on the road. It keeps us in a healthy mindset of doing things right by starting well. Small steps repeated over a long period of time are huge personal leaps.

When my workout partner calls me I know it's "go-time". We both run ¾ of a mile to meet up at a central point. If I end up bailing on him or he bails on me, it's hard to actually follow through with the workout. If he can't make it I have all the right intentions, but for whatever reason I lose the motivation to show up and workout that afternoon. My bond in that workout time is so strong that if he's not there, I make excuses and end up not fitting in the work out. That's how accountability works; we motivate each other and really miss out when we cannot connect.

## KEY INGREDIENTS

Accountability ensures that we don't lie to ourselves or cheat our future hopes and dreams. Healthy accountability is:

- Honest
- Measurable
- Supportive
- Non-Judgmental
- Confidential
- Challenging

Honest accountability cuts to the core of who we are and the purpose we are striving to accomplish. The most important element in accountability is our own ability to not lie to ourselves. Honest accountability doesn't afford us the opportunity to continue to deceive ourselves or the person, coach, group that we are journeying with. Honest accountability means coming to grips with our blind spots, weaknesses, triggers, and asking for help. Accountability that works is not built of false hope, but on living honestly.

We measure our goals so that we can track our progress. Accountability that is measurable is all about taking stock of where we are and laying out small goals along the way that will take us to where we want to be. Setting and sharing deadlines, milestones, benchmarks and targets are essential if accountability is going to work. Making these as simple and clear as possible and revisiting them regularly with you accountability partner, coach, mentor or group is paramount.

As the old saying goes, "No man is an island." The reality of our existence is that we were created for relationship. Simply put, we need each other. This is definitely true when it comes to accountability. If we're going to be successful in our goals we must seek out a person, coach, mentor, or group that is supportive of us and has our best interests in mind. Going it alone doesn't work for the long haul. Positive support affords us the best opportunity to become the people we long to be and provides the encouragement we need to achieve our purpose.

Accountability equals vulnerability. In a real sense it is about asking for help. This is tough for a lot of us. We have been conditioned to be self-sufficient, but if we are deeply honest (which is the first ingredient for healthy accountability) then we have to reach out to folks we can trust. A big part of this is finding a partner, coach, trainer or group that doesn't judge us when we fail, but pushes us to pick ourselves up and try again. We are our own toughest critics, so if accountability is going to work it needs to be with safe people who we can trust that believe in us.

Confidence literally means "with truth." Accountability that is confidential boosts our confidence that we can achieve our goals and accomplish our purpose. Again, it is essential that accountability be built on the truth and not a lie. Accountability partners, coaches, trainers and groups must be a people we can be honest about our past failures, present fears and future dreams. Accountability doesn't work without confidentiality. Honest living is built on relationships that we can trust. A good and purposeful life cannot be built on a lie, it's just not sustainable.

One of the most important elements to accountability is that it has to be challenging. If we are going to grow and change we must be compelled internally and propelled externally. As we talked about in chapter one, the internal compelling comes from discovering a purpose worth fighting for that has to be earned. Healthy accountability happens when our partner, coach, mentor, trainer or group has permission to call us out when we begin to lie to ourselves and challenge us when we aren't giving our best. This isn't pleasant or fun, but it is extremely necessary if we hope to become a better version of ourselves.

# INSIDERS THAT ARE OUTSIDERS

Harvey McKay, a successful businessman and entrepreneur, was once asked his secret for success, his reply: "I have a coach for everything…a business coach, a tennis coach, a writing coach, a speaking coach, a fitness coach." If we want to grow we need the help of others. Coaches, mentors and trainers have the expertise to remind us of the truth we already know, and help us to see what we overlook in our everyday lives. They are an objective voice of hope that spurs us on towards achieving our best.

We pick our friends. We have to let folks know how to hold us accountable. If we need someone to get in our face, or walk beside us it's up to us to let our accountability partners know. We set ourselves up for success when we communicate the best way we receive criticism and feedback. One of the most difficult things to do is to give folks permission to call us out and speak truth into our lives.

According to the American Management Association (AMA) and Institute for Corporate Productivity, *Coaching: A Global Study of Successful Practices,* "…coaching is linked to improved performance and productivity at both the individual and organizational levels." The study goes on to state that organizations that use coaching achieve greater success in raising both individual and organizational performance, particularly when clear rationale about the coaching process is tied to measurable goals.

Finding a good trainer or accountability coach is about finding folks with the right temperament who have credibility and experience in the areas we want to grow in. It pays to do our homework before we start the mentoring/coaching/training process. We must take the time to sit down face to face or go in and work out with the individual to see if they have what we're looking for. It also doesn't hurt to speak with other folks they are working with to find out if they are a good fit for us or not.

Another crucial factor to consider is if the trainer/coach is someone who has our best interests in mind and that exhibits the key ingredients of healthy accountability. Influence is a two-way street and we should be careful who we're letting in and getting close to especially when it comes to this type of voice in our lives. We become like those closest to us and vice-versa so we need to be aware of who we listen to and what advice we follow. Here are a few qualities to look for when seeking outside coaching:

## PERSONALITY

You like your friends because you get along with each other. If you don't like them you're not going to stay on your journey together. Even if they're the best trainer from a knowledge stand-point you still have to like them at the end of the day. Adaptability is important. A good trainer should adapt to the client.

## WALK THE TALK

The leader is the lesson. For us we do 30 minute sessions. 30 minutes is enough. I practice what I preach. I do high-intensity work and preach this to my clients.

## HEART OF A TEACHER

Someone who can really take the time to explain it to you so you can understand it. You have the confidence to do it on your own. Teachers teach you things so that you can go and do it on your own. You can keep progressing.

## SERVANT LEADERSHIP

A matter of doing whatever it takes to meet your needs. A causal conversation leads to personal development. They send you the little extras to make sure that you're a success. Someone who is willing to help you along in this process.

## CONTINUOUS GROWTH

For the trainer. Someone who is on their own journey. A progression of things. They should be introducing new things to you. They shouldn't be stagnant. We should be growing in a training based knowledge. They should be students themselves.

## TRUE PROFESSIONALS

It's not someone who is checking their phone during their session. They treat their training as their career. It's not a side-job. It's doing what they say they are going to do. Starting at a certain time and ending at a certain time. Call, follow-up, that is professional accountability.

## MENTOR NEEDED

While not all of us can afford to hire an expert, all of us have the ability to approach someone we trust or look up to that can act as a mentor to provide much needed accountability in our lives. A quality mentor is not hard to find, if you know where to ask. If we were to think of someone in our life or that we've met who have qualities, values, and characteristics that we admire we could land on the special individual that could potentially help us become a better version of ourselves. This individual is probably a role model that we look up to or have gone to for advice in the past. Finding the courage to tee up a conversation with them could be the key to unlocking our best and finding true accountability.

For the cost of a cup of coffee and 30 minutes of our lives we could connect with a prospective mentor and see if they would be willing to journey with us over the next few months to help us achieve our goals. After a few face-to-face conversations we should be able to determine whether or not the relationship is going to work. Finding someone that we get along with is paramount to our success. Again, finding someone that has our best interests at heart and that isn't afraid to call us out when we need it is essential. Trust is a two way street. We cannot grow without it.

We have to be open and honest with our mentors about our expectations and availability in order to maintain clear communication. Life is busy and both parties are scheduling time to invest in a better future. Healthy boundaries need to be set in order to deal with these expectations. All the essential ingredients apply for healthy accountability in the mentoring relationship. Being realistic from the get-go about our purpose, goals, timelines and stories are all necessary if we hope to get the most out of the mentoring relationship.

Scheduled accountability times are essential as well. Setting up monthly meetings and regular contact via calls and emails are essential to tracking progress, deal with obstacles, and discuss alternative ways to proceed. Mentoring meetings can be over coffee, during a scheduled walk or workout, or over a meal...the main thing is the regularity of getting together for honest conversation and feedback. With a good mentor in place we have the accountability to move towards self-awareness, personal fulfillment, and realizing our health and fitness goals.

## SEEK EXERCISE: *Accountability that Works*

*What is the number one thing holding us back from seeking out accountability?*

*What areas / goals in our lives need the most accountability?*

*Who are three people that we trust to speak into our lives?*

*What would it take for us to reach out to them for their help?*

## AVOIDING ROCK BOTTOM

For me it came through learning. More specifically reading books and listening to leadership talks. When I first started training, I had a client ask me what I listened to in the car when I drove back to Texas. I was a 19 year-old kid with a 10 hour drive home from college. All I listened to was music. He encouraged me to pick up a book on cd. I found Zig Ziggler's, *See You at the Top*, for $40, which at the time was a fortune. I cranked out all 10 CDs on the way home. I listened to those CDs over and over again and it got me fired up. I listened to them so many times I could recite all the stories. That set me on the way of learning about leadership, influence and accountability. I was embarrassed at first when friends would get in my truck and there was some motivational voice on full blast, but eventually I started talking about what I was learning.

We may not always be able to avoid rock bottom, but we can develop the self-discipline to make the right choices. Accountability is the secret ingredient for so many successful people. I am a trainer who needs outside accountability. The main reason that I personally use them is that I know coaches, mentors, and trainers are going to make me better. I know that I cannot do this on my own. In the beginning I tried to do the "lone ranger" approach, but I soon realized that growth can happen a lot faster with the help of others. Hearing other folk's perspectives has benefitted me greatly. I have accountability everywhere I turn in my life. I intentionally seek out people that want to grow. In all my different areas I have support and like-minded folks.

# *Chapter Six:* SEEK: Leveraging Accountability

*"However self-sufficient we may fancy ourselves, we exist only in relation -- to our friend, family, and life partners; to those we teach and mentor; to our co-workers, neighbors, strangers; and even to forces we cannot fully conceive of, let alone define. In many ways, we are our relationships."* — Derrick A. Bell

## Week Six Reading Plan
### Reading / Reflection / Result

**Monday**
- Read Chapter Six

**Tuesday**
- Who is someone in your life that can hold you accountable?

**Wednesday**
- What does healthy accountability look like for you specifically?

**Thursday**
- Re-Read Chapter Six…

**Friday**
- What is your biggest obstacle to achieving your Purpose? Why?

**Saturday**
- What stood out to you the most from this chapter? Why?
- What are you going to do about it?

**Sunday**
- Rest

---

# CHAPTER SEVEN:
# *ENGAGE: Fighting for Others*

*"I alone cannot change the world, but I can cast a stone across the waters to create many ripples."*
— Mother Teresa

When I realized that I wanted to propose to my wife Cassie I did not have enough money to buy a ring. I knew that I didn't want to go into debt to purchase the ring she wanted. I had a connection with a jeweler in town who could make the ring but it had to either be by cash or a check. I was living by my debt-free principle of not putting it on a credit card and I had no real liquid assets. What I did have was my baby…my suped-up truck. Being a hard working single guy from Texas, my truck was a cherished possession. I had dropped quite a bit of money on her at the time. A state of the art sound system, new wheels, and all the little bells and whistles a guy my age could want. I knew that the only shot I had at purchasing the ring was to part ways with my beloved truck.

What wont us guys do for love.

I cleaned the truck up, and put a for sale sign in the back window. It wasn't long before I had an offer from a dad who wanted to purchase the vehicle for his son's first ride. I was able to negotiate the price to cover the cost of the ring and a bike. That's right, I upgraded from four wheels to two. Cassie got the ring she wanted, and I acquired a 6 mile-pedal fest to and from work each day. You see, in life, it's not about saying that we love someone or that we would be willing to do anything to change, it's backing it up with our actions that count. Talk is cheap in love and in life.

Was it worth giving up my most prized possession for her? That's not even worth answering. My choice to sacrifice was no real sacrifice at all. I gained way more in that single moment than I could have ever imagined. I went backwards in order to go forwards. I made jokes at the time about it being this big sacrifice. It was a big deal but it wasn't a big deal. I know it was true to my values.

In that moment of handing the keys over to the guy who was purchasing the truck for his kid, I thought to myself, "This is it. I'm really doing this. This is the point of no return. This is for the rest of my life." When he took the keys, hopped into the drivers seat and drove away, I was both excited and scared all at once. I'm not a total saint. A few mornings when I was making that 6 mile trek into work on my bike, I had to remind myself, that these half-hour sessions of pedaling were worth it. I haven't looked back ever since. It's no wonder they call it engagement. Connecting with another person for a deeper reason, a life lived together and not alone.

Engagement is all about taking the message of this book to other people who need to hear it. Undoubtedly for change to take effect in our lives beyond this week, this month, or even this year we must take the next step and teach that truth to others. If we truly own the message, then we live the message. Living the message means sharing the message with our actions and with our words. Our actions always speak louder than our words.

## SACRIFICE IS WORTH THE PRICE

When we really want something or care about someone, we're willing to sacrifice in order to see that desire become reality. Passion is not just a feeling or a fleeting emotion; it's fuel for this journey called life. Passion requires sacrifice if we truly want to be alive. So few of us live this way. All of us know folks that are searching for a better way to live, a healthier life than the one they have. All of us know someone that needs to hear this message, to see this truth lived out in front of them. Every one of us needs a community to live our purpose and passion out with. When we find that community our purpose and passion takes root and flourishes in our lives.

Real and lasting change never stops with the individual. It always finds its way into the lives of others. When we discover our purpose and begin to move towards becoming a better version of ourselves we cannot help but to influence and impact the lives of those around us. As Malcolm Gladwell once wrote, "If you want to bring a fundamental change in people's belief and behavior...you need to create a community around them, where those new beliefs can be practiced and expressed and nurtured."[1] When we engage those closest to us with intentionality and purpose it changes everyone involved.

Sacrifice literally means, "to give up something for the sake of a better cause." Isn't our personal health and wellness worth giving up desert after every meal? Isn't having the energy and ability to play catch with our kids worth leaving work early for that quality time? Isn't going to bed earlier at night worth the extra energy and rest we need to effectively face our day? Isn't living a life with purpose and meaning worth taking a hard look in the mirror? What we're willing to give up and let go of in life determines the freedom by which we live it.

## THE GOOD FIGHT

Who are we reading this book for? Hopefully, we're reading this book in order to flesh out our purpose and become a better version of ourselves. But, if we want this to be more than just another book on the shelf of our library collecting dust, then we should be thinking about who we know right now that needs to hear this message.

We need to fill in this blank:

*I am going to seek out_____ and share with them the message of this book.*

Who in our life right now is struggling with a reason for making the right choices?

Who in our life right now could use some practical wisdom to unearth purpose and meaning that can sustain them to live a healthier life that matters?

Who in our life right now must read this book?

We all have people in our lives that are literally just making it through. They are comfortable and complacent, adrift in a culture that is built on consumerism and entertainment. We know this to be true because it wasn't so long ago that we were there ourselves. What woke us up? What will wake them up?

## MOTIVATION

Who are we fighting for? Answering this question brings clarity and a way forward. It crystalizes our purpose and gives us the motivation to continue on the road less traveled. For me it's my wife, my daughters, my team and my clients. I have had a goal from way back in my early days of coaching soccer. I would see countless parents at soccer practices and their kids' games and I knew that they could not play with their kids. They couldn't run around and mix it up with them and play a game if their life depended on it. That started etching into my mind the realization that I wanted to be in good enough shape that I could always play with (and hopefully beat) my kids in sports until they were 18. I hope that I have enough 'play' left in me to go out and take them on.

I am also motivated to practice what I preach with my clients. I feel a deep responsibility to keep myself in shape for them. The definition of impact is, ' the effect or impression of one thing on another.' Every time I connect with my clients, whether it's on the gym floor or out in the local restaurant, I want to live such a life that it positively impacts and affects them. My life has to match my message. In a real sense I try to live by the principle that the leader is the lesson. My life is the greatest testimony, the loudest message, and the most powerful tool that I have to impact and influence my clients.

Engagement is all about commitment. It's saying yes to the one thing that can actually bring life to our circumstances, our communities, ourselves. When we engage those in our lives that genuinely need it we are not just offering a lifeline to them, but to ourselves. When we reach out we're grabbing a hand that needs us, and we're also clutching a hand that we need. When we share why we're consciously making changes to live a life of purpose, we are choosing to go against the flow in a culture that is after the latest fad. Living a life of purpose isn't about reinventing the wheel, as much as it about getting back to the basics of why we have a wheel in the first place.

## FAMILIAR VOICES

When I close my eyes and think back on the people who have shaped an informed my life the most I cannot help but hear and see my Grandpa and the way he taught my brothers and me the right way to do things. He was truly a voice of innovation and perseverance in my life. The way he worked and overcame obstacles, his sheer will to come back after suffering a heart attack and beating the doctor's odds more than made an impression on me. His is a voice that lives on in my own life.

When we think back on the people that have influenced us the most, it is those few voices that we can still hear ringing in our hearts. Those voices encouraged us to not give up, to keep fighting the good fight, to carry on no matter the cost, and to finish what we started. These voices of hope are familiar and what they said lit a spark within our hearts and minds to become better human beings. These voices stay with us, because they meant and mean something. They are voices of truth, correction, challenge, and hope. Those words spoken at the right time took root in the very core of whom we are and are still shaping us today.

## CLARIFYING PURPOSE

In the first chapter, *Planning*, of this book we looked at the power of legacy and need to set healthy goals. We did this by asking two very important questions:

1) What legacy do we want to leave behind?
2) How can being fit and healthy help us achieve this legacy?

Honestly answering these questions was the first step in becoming a better version of ourselves and understanding our purpose.

Looking back 6 short weeks ago, what goals did we set to begin to achieve this legacy? Why?

What sacrifices did we make to achieve them?

Who in our lives has been impacted by our choice to take action?

When we take the first step, it naturally leads to taking another step. When we set a simple, clear and measurable goal and reach that goal, we gain the courage to continue to set new goals. When we repeat this over time we end up living a life that encourages others to do the same. Our courage to set goals, takes steps, and make changes impacts and influences those around us. That's why it's so important for us to not only pay attention to those who need to hear this message, but to actively reach out to them and engage them right where they are at. It's said that teaching is the greatest act of optimism. When we teach others we are actually giving them permission to take healthy risks. We become a voice of hope in their lives and we strengthen our own purpose-filled journey.

## RETHINKING FOOD

In the second chapter, *Understanding* we examined the importance of changing our behavior in order to change our diet. We asked ourselves *why* we eat what we eat. This clear understanding of our relationship with food enabled us to move towards sustained healthy choices and living when it comes to our food choices. Taking stock of our lives (and refrigerators) has helped us come up with a simple plan that was achievable in our pursuit of being fit and healthy.

Who in our lives could directly benefit from our newfound knowledge and relationship with food?

Who in our lives needs help cleaning out their pantry or refrigerator?

Who in our lives needs us to encourage them to start eating real whole food?

Self-discipline is a by-product of self-awareness, and that is why real and lasting change happens when we act on what we know about ourselves at the deepest part of who we are as individuals. When we are fit and healthy we will have the energy and mindset to live a life of purpose and leave a legacy of impact. We will also naturally talk to others about rethinking their own food choices and how those daily decisions positive affect the rest of their lives.

## MAXIMIZING ENERGY

In chapter three, *Recharging*, we looked at the importance of living a healthy rhythm of life in order to live with purpose and leave a legacy of significance and meaning for the next generation. This meant counting the cost and understanding what personal discipline was all about. We looked at how busy we are and our need to refuel by unplugging from the franticness of life.

Who in our life is too busy?

Who in our life needs to slow down before they burn out?

Who in our life needs to know that it's okay if a few plates stop spinning?

Engaging these individuals with a message of rest and refueling will not be easy, but we now know that we can only finish strong by getting the right amount of sleep at night, by engaging in activities that refuel us, and by slowing down. When we choose to live at a healthy rhythm of life, we are giving them permission and an example to follow.

## INFUSING JOY

*Play* was the subject of the fourth chapter, and it was all about the power of infusing joy into everyday life. We learned that infusing joy was about more than evoking an emotion, and more about possessing what we desire, especially when it comes to achieving our health and fitness goals. We discovered that infusing joy in our everyday lives enables us to set simple goals, and work hard to achieve them without burning out before we reach the finish line.

Who in our lives right now is taking themselves too seriously?

Who in our lives right now needs to learn to laugh more?

Who in our lives right now should we hang out with before they burn out?

Infusing joy is probably the most effective way to engage others. Who doesn't want to have a good time while at the same time become a better version of themselves? Joy is contagious and should be the quality of our relationships with folks that need to hear this message. Infusing joy is about laughing out loud with people who are on the journey with us. Infusing joy is about having some serious fun as we create a better world and live a legacy worth replicating.

## EMBRACING RESPONSIBILITY

In *Organize,* chapter five, we looked at how we are wired. So many people we are connected with really need to read this chapter, because self-awareness is paramount to living a life of purpose and leaving a legacy of significance. If we really believe that our ability to live an organized life is directly related to our ability to come to grips with who we are and how we prefer to structure the daily details life throws at us. then we'll help others to do the same.

Which Explorers in our lives could benefit from a bit of organization?

Which Planners in our lives could benefit from appreciating Explorers more?

How has our own preference for organizing life affected our personal relationships?

Who should we have the Organize conversation with?

When we understand our preference for Planning and Exploring we are light years ahead of the masses that stumble and speed ahead without the clarity and self-awareness of discovering a life of Purpose. By sharing and clarifying how we're wired, we'll enable others to embrace their own preferences and take the next step towards their health and fitness goals.

## LEVERAGING ACCOUNTABILITY

In *Seek,* chapter six, we explored the reason why we cannot afford to go it alone if we truly want to live a life of purpose. We saw that accountability equals vulnerability. In a real sense it is about asking for help. This is probably the most intimate and challenging of all the aspects to achieving our purpose for that very reason. All meaningful relationships are built on trust. If we are going to truly engage others with this message, we have to be people that can be trusted. Our lives have to match our message.

Who in our lives right now could use healthy accountability?

Who in our lives right now could benefit from reaching out for a coach or mentor?

What would it look like to have that depth of relationship with that individual?

Accountability cannot be forced, however it can be exemplified. When we are open and honest bout our need for others feedback and wisdom it creates an opportunity to share the message of this book. When we are vulnerable it opens the door for others to reach out and open up. How many folks do we know that avoid this level of relationship? It comes at a cost, but the benefit far outweighs the discomfort of folks knowing the good, bad, ugly and beautiful story that is ours. Who knows, they might even embrace that within themselves if we would have the courage to go there first.

## THE JOURNEY AND THE DESTINATION

"The strongest influences in my life and my work are always whomever I love. Whomever I love and am with most of the time, or whomever I remember most vividly. I think that's true of everyone, don't you?" - Tennessee Williams quotes (American playwright. 1911-1983)

I am literally with my wife almost 24/7. We work together, play together, shop together, eat together, parent together and still only have one car. I wouldn't want it any other way. She is that constant voice of hope no matter what state of mind I'm in. When things are going great and things are going south, she is a rock and an honest voice in my life. More than anything, I want her to see that I am continually becoming a better Brent. For me, when I think about it, her words and her thoughts of me make me want to try harder, to be better, to work on whatever I need to work on. Honestly, for me I am striving to leave a legacy for her and our girls. It makes no sense for me to conquer the world and lose them. I want to be healthy for them. I want to continuously get better for them. I hope that my life would clearly exhibit that I will not settle for less, because they deserve my best. I am fighting for Cassie and my girls.

## ULTIMATE THINGS

The most powerful thing we do in life is make choices. No matter how big or small the decision, they affect the very trajectory and quality of our lives. When we consciously choose to engage others and share how discovering our purpose has benefitted our own lives, we will undoubtedly be paying it forward and then some. Our lives and their lives will never be the same.

The hardest part is to not give up once we decide to live according to the legacy that we hope to leave behind. Armed with clear goals and the courage to do the next right thing, we cannot help but to slowly change our world. Self-discipline is not easy, but the really good things in life are never easy. What matters most is that we continue on this path towards wholeness and health guided by clear, measurable goals, and a desire to not give in to the status quo. It's not easy to say no, or to set boundaries, or to unplug and pull away to gain some perspective, but in the long run it's the small things that add up to make a big difference.

When we make the decision to do the right thing, and share openly about the difference that it has made in our lives, we will undoubtedly impact and influence future generations. This book is for the influencers, the game-changers, the coaches, teachers, and parents that are responsible for the little ones who are our future. Their eyes are on us, and ultimately, it is up to us to make positive choices to impact and guide them along the right path.

When we're tempted to throw in the towel and give into apathy, we just need to think about those who are looking up to us, counting on us to show them what real life is about. Then most difficult part is to step up and take ownership for the choices we're making. When we do, our children notice.


## THE TABLE

The dinner table is a great place to start engaging others with purpose and passion. For generations, families and friends have gathered together to break bread and fellowship with one another. What would it look like if the meal we were sharing was healthy for us? What would it look like if our conversation was seasoned with words that bring life? What if we rediscovered the power of the small sacred space in our homes? Again, it's a small choice to make to put away the TV trays and sit facing one another.

I truly believe that if we made this one small choice it would revolutionize all of our relationships. Think about it for just a moment. By making dinner time a part of the rhythm of our daily lives, we're engaging those folks most dear to us and teaching them every single topic we've covered in this book. When we sit down together for a meal we're making a statement. We're saying that we belong, that we matter. When we gather for a healthy meal together we're also saying that the food we eat matters. When we sit down to a meal together, we're also consciously slowing down and interrupting the hectic pace of our day. When we sit down to a meal together, undoubtedly we'll be sharing stories and joy with one another. When we sit down at the table it brings order to our lives. When we sit down with family and friends and are open and honest, accountability is a natural component of our conversation. We can pay attention to one another and debrief our day. When we sit down with one another, we are undoubtedly engaging in community. One small choice. One big difference.

So what are we waiting for? Are we going to choose to live a life of purpose and leave a legacy of significance? Life is short, let's start small. Let's start now.

# *Chapter Seven:* ENGAGE: Fighting for Others

*"Devote yourself to loving others, devote yourself to your community around you, and devote yourself to creating something that gives you purpose and meaning."* — Mitch Albom

## <u>Week Seven Reading Plan</u>
### Reading / Reflection / Result

**Monday**
- Read Chapter Seven

**Tuesday**
- Who in your life needs to hear the message of this book?

**Wednesday**
- How can being fit and healthy help them become a better version of themselves?

**Thursday**
- Re-Read Chapter Seven…

**Friday**
- What is your biggest obstacle to achieving your Purpose? Why?

**Saturday**
- What stood out to you the most from this chapter? Why?
- What are you going to do about it?

**Sunday**
- Rest

# References

1. http://www.who.int/mediacentre/factsheets/fs311/en/
2. http://www.who.int/mediacentre/factsheets/fs311/en/
3. http://www.census.gov/main/www/popclock.html
4. http://www.reuters.com/article/2012/04/30/us-obesity-idUSBRE83T0C820120430
5. http://www.forbes.com/sites/davidmaris/2012/06/01/bloombergs-not-so-happy-meal/
6. http://www.etymonline.com/index.php?term=goal
7. http://www.redorbit.com/news/health/2045046/us_weight_loss_market_worth_609_billion/
8. http://usatoday30.usatoday.com/news/nation/story/2012/09/19/state-obesity-rates-could-skyrocket-by-2030/57799906/1
9. http://www.hsph.harvard.edu/obesity-prevention-source/obesity-consequences/economic/
10. http://www.seattleorganicrestaurants.com/vegan-whole-foods/family-farm-lands/
11. http://www.livestrong.com/article/493628-much-sugar-allowance-day/
12. http://www.cancer.gov/statistics
13. http://www.prnewswire.com/news-releases/shopsmart-poll-57-percent-of-women-say-cost-of-food-keeps-them-from-eating-healthy-151343115.html
14. http://www.thenhf.com/article.php?id=2514
15. http://savethewater.org/tag/water-quality/
16. http://www.nature.com/ejcn/journal/v57/n2s/full/1601898a.html
17. http://www.caringonline.com/eatdis/reports/hydration/index.htm
18. http://dash.harvard.edu/bitstream/handle/1/8852186/Wolf.html?sequence=2
19. http://www.med.navy.mil/sites/nmcsd/Patients/Pages/

PortionDistortion-ServingSizesareGrowing.aspx

20. http://www.usda.gov/factbook/chapter2.pdf

21. http://news.blogs.cnn.com/2012/08/22/40-
of-u-s-food-wasted-report-says/
comment-page-2/

22. http://www.salon.com/2012/03/14/
bring_back_the_40_hour_work_week/

23. http://usatoday30.usatoday.com/money/jobcenter/workplace/
story/2012-04-15/workers-sue-unpaid-overtime/54301774/1

24. http://www.worksmart.org.uk/
news/2011/06/40-hour-week-burnout-risk

25. http://www.motherjones.com/politics/2011/06/
speed-up-american-workers-long-hours

26. http://experiencelife.com/article/getting-to-sleep/

27. http://www.acoem.org/uploadedFiles/Public_Affairs/Policies_
And_Position_Statements/Fatigue%20Risk%20Management%20
in%20the%20Workplace.pdf

28. http://www.myersbriggs.org/my-mbti-personality-type/my-mbti-
results/how-frequent-is-my-type.asp

29. http://www.myersbriggs.org/my-mbti-personality-type/mbti-
basics/extraversion-or-introversion.asp

30. http://www.myersbriggs.org/my-mbti-personality-type/mbti-
basics/extraversion-or-introversion.asp

31. Gladwell, Malcolm. Outliers: The Story of Success. New York:
Little, Brown and Co., 2008.

32. http://edition.cnn.com/2012/10/17/health/health-naps-brain

33. http://news.health.com/2012/10/17/
power-naps-may-boost-right-brain-activity/

34. http://www.merriam-webster.com/dictionary/passion

35. http://www.nimh.nih.gov/health/publications/depression/com-
plete-index.shtml

36. http://www.mayoclinic.com/health/exercise-and-stress/SR00036

37. Wilson, Penny. The Playwork Primer, 2010 Edition.

38. http://well.blogs.nytimes.com/2012/08/01/
dieting-vs-exercise-for-weight-loss/

39. Ibid.

40. http://www.cheori.org/en/newsreleases?newsid=323

41. Ibid

42. http://www.merriam-webster.com/dictionary/joy

43.  Franklin, Benjamin. The Autobiography of Benjamin Franklin. The Macmillan Publishing Co, Copyright 1962.

44. http://www.merriam-webster.com/dictionary/grateful

45. http://www.cdc.gov/nchs/fastats/deaths.htm

46. http://www.ihrsa.org/media-center/2011/4/5/us-health-club-membership-exceeds-50-million-up-108-industry.html

47. http://www.statisticbrain.com/gym-membership-statistics/

48. http://www.merriam-webster.com/dictionary/blame

49. http://www.alincoln-library.com/abraham-lincoln-quotes.shtml

50. http://www.goodreads.com/quotes/299032-i-long-to-accomplish-a-great-and-noble-task-but

51. http://www.startribune.com/business/188309941.html

52. http://www.amanet.org/news/191.aspx

53. Gladwell, Malcolm. The Tipping Point: How Little Things Can Make a Big Difference. Little Brown and Co, Copyright 2000.

## Purpose Online Resources

Since this is not your typical fitness book - loaded with smiling and super fit individuals showing you basic exercises, a step-by-step training plan, a magical daily meal program, and an approved grocery shopping list - I thought I'd provide some bonus online resources to help you along on your journey. I will keep adding to *Purpose* by putting a ton of great material online regularly. So come check us out online at **www.BrentGallagher.com.**

## 'Build a Better U' App

Build A Better U is an original training and social app that gets you ripped in seven short weeks. This is one of the best conditioning apps in the App Store. Connect with certified trainer Brent Gallagher as he pushes you to be the best version of yourself possible. Are the workouts not hard enough for you? You can connect with Brent for additional customized one on one training through the app. Search - *Build a Better U*

## More on Brent Gallagher

To have Brent Gallagher speak to your organization about the principles found in *Purpose, email cassie@WestUFit.com*

## What's Your #Purpose

Connect with Brent and the *#Purpose* community of individuals who are simply striving to become better versions of themselves:

- Facebook: BrentGallagherWUF
- Twitter: BrentGallagher
- Blog: BrentGallagher.com/Blog

CPSIA information can be obtained at www.ICGtesting.com
Printed in the USA
BVOW07s0815300114

343362BV00003B/467/P